BARRON'S PARENTING KEYS

KEYS TO PREPARING & CARING FOR YOUR NEWBORN

William Sears, M.D.

Pediatrician
Assistant Clinical Professor of Pediatrics
at the University of Southern California

D0815717

BARRON'S

New York • London • Toronto • Sydney

Copyright © 1991 by Barron's Educational Series, Inc.

All inquiries should be addressed to:
Barron's Educational Series, Inc.
250 Wireless Boulevard
Hauppauge, New York 11788

Library of Congress Catalog Card No. 90-25847

International Standard Book No. 0-8120-4539-4

Library of Congress Cataloging-in-Publication Data

Sears, William, M.D.
  Keys to preparing and caring for your newborn / by William Sears.
    p. cm.
  ISBN 0-8120-4539-4
  1. Infants (Newborn)—Care. I. Title.
RJ253.S4   1991
649'.122—dc20   90-25847
                                      CIP

PRINTED IN THE UNITED STATES OF AMERICA
5 6 7 8   5500   6 5 4 3 2

TABLE OF CONTENTS

	Introduction	1
1	Selecting a Parenting Style That Works for You	3
2	Choosing Where to Birth Your Baby	8
3	Childbirth Classes	12
4	Bonding with Your Preborn Baby	15
5	Mothering Your Preborn Child	17
6	Choosing Whether to Breastfeed or Formula-Feed	21
7	Breastfeeding—Right-Start Techniques	23
8	Bonding with Your Newborn Baby	26
9	Rooming in with Your Newborn	33
10	What Newborns Look Like	38
11	Newborn Reflexes	41
12	Routine Tests, Injections, and Medications	45
13	Early Newborn Changes	49
14	Nest in with Your Baby	56
15	Choosing the Right Formula for Your Baby	59
16	Deciding Whether to Have Your Baby Circumcised	65
17	Naming Your Baby	70
18	What Newborns Can See	73
19	What Newborns Can Hear	77
20	The Newborn's Cry	81
21	Understanding Your Newborn's Temperament	84
22	Fear of Spoiling	87
23	Selecting a Baby Carrier	90
24	Selecting a Safe Crib	95
25	Outfitting the Layette and Nursery	98

26   Your Baby's Medical Checkups   101
27   Common Newborn Medical Concerns   104
28   Common Skin Problems in the Newborn   107
29   Caring for Your Newborn's Bodily Needs   112
30   Introducing the New Baby to Siblings   117
31   Infant Stimulation   120
32   Parenting the Hospitalized Newborn   124
33   Recognizing When Your Newborn is Seriously Ill   127
34   Postpartum Depression   130
35   Parenting the Adopted Newborn   133
36   Parenting the Handicapped Newborn   135
37   Single Mothering the Newborn   138
38   Traveling With Your Newborn   141
39   Returning to Work   145
40   Marriage Adjustments to the New Baby   148
     Questions and Answers   151
     Glossary   164
     Index   166

INTRODUCTION

The quality of the interaction between you as parents and your newborn baby sets the tone for your parenting career. The material in *Keys to Preparing and Caring for Your Newborn* is designed to help parents get off to a good start, with a sense of completeness, a rightness that brings out the best in both parents and baby. In the early weeks of parenting, well-meaning friends and family will bombard you with advice on how to care for your baby and eagerly share with you their personal lists of "how tos." But it's your baby, not someone else's. Learning how to care for your baby means developing an overall parenting style that allows the important "how tos" to follow naturally.

The style of parenting that best helps parents and baby fit together is what I call "attachment parenting," described in Key 1. If you follow its principles, I believe you will get to know your baby, help your baby feel right, and truly enjoy your child.

The information for this book has been gathered from my experiences as former director of a university hospital newborn nursery and associate ward chief of the newborn ward at the Hospital for Sick Children in Toronto, the largest children's hospital in the world. In addition, I have had nearly 20 years in pediatric practice, during which I have counseled thousands of parents on the care of their newborns. Not least, I am father of seven children.

In *Keys to Preparing and Caring for Your Newborn,* I wish to provide practical tools for arriving at a style of parenting that works for you. I hope that by using these tools, parents will improve their powers of observation as keen baby watchers, get to know their newborn's individual preferences and capabilities, and come to believe that the 90s are a good time to be a parent or a baby.

1

^^

SELECTING A PARENTING STYLE THAT WORKS FOR YOU

This book is based on the premise that the key to a successful relationship between parents and child is what I call "fit"—a sense of completeness in a relationship, a coming together as a family. Achieving a good fit is an outgrowth of every decision you as prospective and then new parents make about your child—where he will be born, what name you will bestow, what you as a pregnant woman eat, how you will respond to your newborn's cues, a response that in turn helps the newborn learn how to communicate more effectively what his needs are. The growth of this kind of give-and-take creates a bond between parent and child that naturally develops depth and harmony over time—in short, fit.

Because of the wide variety of family circumstances, the variability of individual mothers and fathers, and the different need levels of their babies, there is a wide variety of parenting styles. During my 20 years of pediatric practice I have observed all sorts of parenting styles and have practiced different styles of parenting my own seven children. The style that helps most growing families to come together as a family is a style I call attachment parenting. The elements of attachment parenting are:

1. **Be open to the cues of your baby and respond according to your intuitive feelings.** Part of

developing a fit during the early weeks is to match the need level of the baby and the response level of the parents. Baby gives a cue and the mother and father, because they are open and tuned into the baby, respond to the cue. In time the communication network is in harmony.

2. **Respond promptly to your baby's cries.** A baby's cry is designed to guarantee the survival of the baby and the development of the parents. Unresponsiveness disturbs the fit. By allowing yourself a natural response to your baby's cry and not a restrained response, you learn to respond better, and your baby learns to "cry better," as it were—to cue you in to his or her needs. Beware of those ubiquitous advice-givers who unintentionally disturb the fit, telling you to "let her cry it out" or that "he's just exercising his lungs." It is very easy for someone to advise letting someone else's baby cry. They are not tuned to *your* baby. They are outside the fit.

3. **Feed on cue and not on schedule.** I wish to replace the term schedule with "harmony," for I know of no other biological interaction that contributes more to the fit than nursing on cue. I use the term "nursing" to mean not only breastfeeding but, in a broader sense, "comforting." Cue-feeding, which is gradually replacing the older term "demand-feeding," encourages you to watch your baby for signs of hunger, instead of watching the clock or some other outside schedule that has little to do with your baby's needs.

4. **Wear your baby.** One of the most important changes in recent parenting styles is that more

babies are "worn" than "wheeled." Wearing your baby means changing a stereotypéd view of a newborn as a separate person. You may feel that your baby is a separate person, but she may not feel that way! The womb continues, birth having changed only the matter in which the womblike environment is expressed. Holding your baby a lot of the time means changing attitudes toward holding babies. Some new parents feel that they should hold their baby just long enough to comfort her and then put her down, that holding periods are no more than dutiful intervals between feed ings. Research has shown that carrying babies is not just a fashionable trend; it actually benefits infant behavior and infant development—carried babies cry 50 percent less and show enhanced visual alertness.

5. **Share sleep with your baby.** This style of nighttime parenting allows the daytime fitting-in to be extended into the night. I personally believe that parents should be open to trying various sleeping arrangements. Babies usually give parents clues as to where they sleep the best. Some babies sleep best in their own cribs in their own rooms; others sleep best in a bed in their parents' room; many babies, I believe, sleep best in their parents' bed. Where all three of you sleep the best is the right arrangement for you. The concept of sharing sleep (baby, mother, and father in the same bed) is gradually becoming a more common style of nighttime parenting in the West; it has, of course, been the accepted style in other parts of the world for years.

These attachment styles are not directed at benefiting the baby or the parent so much as they benefiting the *interaction* between parent and infant in the following ways:

1. Attachment parenting improves your sensitivity. Upon first glance you may consider the attachment style of parenting as all giving, giving, giving. To a certain extent it is. However, there is another side to the equation. The more parents give to the baby, the more the baby gives back to the parents. Mutual giving is part of the fit. For example, when a mother breastfeeds, holds, and caresses her baby and responds to her baby's cry, she gives the baby both nourishment and comfort. The baby, in turn, gives something back to the mother. In response to these attachment stimuli, the mother produces a hormone called prolactin, perhaps the biological basis for "mother's intuition." In a very real sense, then, the baby "gives" to the mother the very hormone which helps her to "mother" him.

   This mutual giving is beautifully illustrated in breastfeeding an infant to sleep, a parenting style I call "nursing down." Mother gives to her baby her milk, which contains a sleep-inducing substance only recently discovered by physicians. Meanwhile, the suckling baby stimulates mother to produce more prolactin, which exerts a tranquilizing effect on the mother. Thus, mother helps put the baby to sleep, and the baby helps put mother to sleep. The biological effects may be summed up in one word—"sensitivity."

2. Attachment parenting helps babies (and parents) to thrive. All infants grow; not all infants thrive.

Thriving takes growth one step further—it is growth to one's fullest potential. New research in experimental animals shows that infants attached to their mothers show a higher level of growth hormone and higher levels of enzymes that promote brain growth. Perhaps the reason that these infants thrive is due to the organizing effect of this style of parenting. Infants who are carried more cry less and are likely to be more visually and aurally attentive. They spend more time in the state of quiet alertness, in which they interact best with their environment.

3. Attachment parenting helps organize the baby. The newborn baby is naturally disorganized. His movements are random and jerky. Most of his cues seem purposeless and hard to decode. Baby's sleep/wake cycles are exhaustingly irregular. However, current research shows that infants who spend most of their days in close proximity to their mothers develop more organized sleep/wake cycles than do newborns who spend the majority of time separated from their mothers.

Won't so much interaction "spoil" the infant? New research is finally put the spoiling theory on the shelf forever. Parental responsiveness actually fosters security and independence; it does not "spoil" a baby.

The five attachment styles suggested above are the early tools that can help parents get off to the right start with their baby. From these basic tools you can branch off into a parenting style that fits best with your own preferences, your lifestyle, and the temperament of your baby, all leading to the ultimate goal in parenting—really enjoying your baby.

2

~~~~~~

CHOOSING WHERE TO BIRTH YOUR BABY

The joyous announcement "Honey, we're pregnant!" naturally brings with it important choices. In addition to choosing the right obstetrician and pediatrician, you need to decide on the birthing environment. Today's expectant couples have many options in childbirth, or Alternative Birthing Concepts—the ABCs of modern obstetrics. These alternative birthing concepts involve more than just different physical facilities; they represent the increasing mutual respect among the hospital, the obstetrician, the pediatrician, and the parents. These alternatives recognize that childbirth is not a disease and that couples should have choices in the procedures that are done during their child's birth.

Traditional delivery methods. I mention this option only to discourage it. Until recent years a delivering mother was managed like a surgical patient. She was admitted to a labor room, usually a small, unattractive facility that was not conducive to helping labor progress. As the time of delivery became imminent mother was wheeled to a delivery room which resembled a sterile operating room. Mother even delivered baby on an operating room table. Following delivery mother was wheeled into a recovery room to recover from the "operation." Baby, meanwhile, was placed in a plastic box (a bassinet) and wheeled to the nursery to join other babies in plastic boxes. Mother and baby were then reunited after both had recovered from the trauma of birth.

The LDR concept. The newest option, one that I highly recommend, is the facility in which mother and father enter one room to Labor, Deliver, and Recover (LDR). Baby stays with the mother from birth to discharge from the hospital and is taken to the nursery only if medical complications occur. This room, pleasant and bright, contains a rocking chair, many windows, a lounge chair, and an adjustable "bedroom" bed to make delivery easier. All the necessary medical and surgical equipment are unobtrusively but efficiently placed around the room.

LDR rooms are not passing fads but a growing reality. They are here to stay because, in addition to making birth more enjoyable, they are simply better medicine. I have noticed that mothers delivering in an LDR room progress more efficiently and that birth is less traumatic for both mother and baby. Mothers progress better because they are encouraged to move around during labor and assume whatever position is the most comfortable, making them feel more relaxed, more at home. Any attending family also feels more at home. Ask your obstetrician which hospitals offer the LDR concept. All hospitals that wish to stay in the baby business will have it.

If you or your doctor anticipate a high-risk delivery, choose a hospital that has a neonatal intensive care unit (NICU)—a medical unit staffed by neonatologists, experts trained to care for sick newborns. This is much better medicine than having to transport an ill newborn, such as a premature baby, from the place of birth to a facility with a NICU. In fact, many hospitals that do not have a NICU routinely transfer a laboring mother whose child may need one to a hospital with such a unit. Mothers make much better incubators than ambulances do.

Birthing centers. Birthing centers are another fairly new option for expectant couples. These buildings are adjacent to or near a hospital. They are staffed by certified nurses or midwives and are sometimes operated by obstetricians. If the birthing center is owned and operated by midwives, there is obstetrical backup. Every room in a birthing center follows the LDR concept. A good birthing center screens prospective clients very carefully and accepts only mothers without identifiable obstetrical risk. Their main benefit is that they are staffed by midwives, a wonderful woman-to-woman support that is lacking in most hospitals. You should ask certain questions as you decide whether to use a birthing center and seek one that is appropriate for you: Do you have any obstetrical risk factors such as multiple pregnancy, possible prematurity, or diabetes? Are the midwives properly credentialed? Is there adequate obstetrical backup in case of unexpected problems during delivery? Is there a routine set-up for immediate transport to the hospital?

Home births. The home birth movement arose because the traditional system of maternal care failed to recognize a genuine consumer need. An increasing number of couples have reacted to the childbirth-is-a-disease-needing-treatment-by-an-operation attitude by taking birth back into the home. Because of the possibility of obstetrical complications, both the American Academy of Obstetrics and Gynecology and the American Academy of Pediatrics advise against giving birth at home. The person who has the highest risk, the baby, has no voice in this decision. I am in deep sympathy with couples who wish to give birth at home, and I can speak with some insight into this dilemma, having attended several such home births. It is a beautiful human experience for parents and babies. It is vital, however, that mothers be **properly selected** and the birth **properly attended.** The mother should have absolutely no risk factors that require medical attention, and no problems, such as infection or prematurity, should be expected with the baby. Unfortunately, many complications with the baby cannot be identified until after the birth. Proper attendance at the birth means the presence of qualified birthing attendants, usually certified midwives. At present, the health care delivery system in the United States is not set up for home birthing. In countries where home birthing is widely practiced and where there is adequate obstetrical and hospital backup, home birthing is no riskier than hospital birthing. Perhaps the day will come when hospitals and homes everywhere can deliver a safe obstetrical system for parents.

Water laboring. Among the most recent innovations in making birth easier for women is laboring in water. Actually, this obstetrical practice has been done in other countries for years, although it is relatively new in the West. During labor mother sits in body-temperature water in a large tub resembling a Jacuzzi. The water's buoyancy makes it easier for the mother to support her body and endure the contractions. The birthing muscles are more relaxed; mother's labor progresses better. Because a mother is able to freely move around the tub, she is able to assume a position most comfortable for her. The medical benefits of such practice have been well documented in birthing centers that encourage it.

In our family of seven we have experienced all of the birthing environments described above. The obstetrical facilities of the future, and one which I hope most mothers will choose, contain the best parts of all of them: An LDR concept, birth attended by midwives, obstetrical backup, laboring in water, with the birthing unit adjacent to a newborn intensive care unit. The newest and most successful obstetrical units now incorporate these characteristics. They are good for the mother, good for the baby, and constitute good medicine.

3

‌‌‌‌‌‌‌‌‌‌‌‌‌‌‌‌‌‌‌‌‌‌‌‌‌‌‌‌‌‌‌‌‌‌‌

CHILDBIRTH CLASSES

Just as there are many options in birthing environments, there are many options in childbirth classes. You should choose one that is independent of any hospital in order to have an overview of the many childbirth options. Hospital-based classes prepare you to be a "good patient." The organizations with the most experience in teaching childbirth classes are the International Childbirth Education Association (ICEA), the American Academy of Husband-Coached Childbirth (the Bradley Method), and the American Society for Psychoprophylaxis in Obstetrics (ASPO—the Lamaze Method).

Here are some general guidelines for choosing the class that is right for you. Examine the experience of the instructor. Has she experienced birth herself? Is she up-to-date on all the options of childbirth? Is she active and involved as a labor support person herself? Get references from friends and acquaintances. Is the time and location of the class convenient for you? Also examine the class content. Avoid classes or methods that use external gimmicks, such as focusing on dangling trinkets, to teach you to escape from your body; these are unrealistic and easily forgotten during the heightened excitement of labor. The topics included in a good childbirth class include prenatal exercises, relaxation techniques, proper breathing, physiology of pregnancy and birth, comforting measures, medications and procedures, and specific instructions on how the laboring couple can work together to ease the discomfort and speed labor's progress. A good childbirth class can teach you how to listen to your body—

to know when to move, to stay still, to sit, to squat, to balance, to lie on all fours, and to walk around. Alternative childbirth environments such as LDR rooms, sibling visitations, and bonding and rooming-in, are covered. Nutrition is emphasized; things to be avoided during pregnancy are discussed. A good class usually provides a lending library and presents slides or films showing labor, birth, and the events surrounding it. Breastfeeding information and discussion of life with a new baby are important. Postpartum adjustment, physical and emotional, can be a big shock to first-time parents, so some discussion and sharing in this area is important.

Childbirth classes are beginning to place less emphasis on the role of father as a labor coach. Men simply do not relate empathetically to the emotional and physical changes of the laboring woman. It is better for the father to leave the technical matters to a labor support person; he has a very important role of another kind. He can embrace his wife, rub her back, walk with her, give her chips and fluids, and even guard against commotion.

What is a labor support person? This Old World custom is one of the newest entries into making childbirth easier for mothers. A labor support person is a mother with some mid-wifery and/or obstetrical nursing experience. She is trained to support the laboring mother during childbirth, helping her move with the flow of her body, and to recognize and act on her own body signals and generally helping labor progress more efficiently and less uncomfortably. Studies have shown that mothers who are assisted by a labor support person have shorter and less traumatic labors. A labor support person (also called a *doula*) also takes pressure off the father.

I advise couples to take their childbirth class seriously, giving it top priority in their schedules. Becoming thoroughly and competently prepared for the birth of a child yields benefits out of all proportion to the time invested.

In addition to childbirth classes, it is helpful to join a support group during your pregnancy. The information you receive and the friends you make often carry over into helpful parenting support during your first years as parents. Of the many parenting organizations, the oldest and largest, and the one I recommend, is the La Leche League International (LLLI). This is a volunteer women's organization whose leaders have special training and years of parenting experience. Although LLLI was begun primarily to advocate and promote breastfeeding, it is an excellent support group that teaches good parenting styles, even for mothers who choose not to breastfeed or who are not able to. There are League groups in nearly every major city throughout the United States and throughout the world. You can find the location of your nearest group by calling 1-800-LaLeche.

You should join LLLI during the third trimester of your pregnancy and attend their meetings. In addition to receiving helpful information and making supportive friends, you'll receive a wealth of practical advice and have access to an up-to-date lending library of books and references on parenting and childbirth. In my experience, parents in LLLI have one thing in common: They enjoy their children. This is a group of professional parents teaching new parents. Take advantage of what they have to offer.

In addition to LLLI, you may find valuable support groups and parent education classes at your local YMCA, hospital, or church. Attend as many of these group meetings as time and energy allow. Select from each group the information that best fits your own lifestyle and the style of parenting you are most comfortable with.

4

BONDING WITH YOUR
PREBORN BABY

Throughout this book I stress the concept of harmony with your newborn as one of the best ways to get into parenting. This harmony begins during pregnancy. A new and exciting field of research, called fetal awareness, is investigating the impact of the emotional state of the mother during the last months of pregnancy on the emotional development of the baby. Recent research suggests that when a pregnant mother becomes anxious or stressed, the level of her stress hormones (adrenalin and cortisone) increases. These hormones cross the placenta into the fetal circulatory system and may agitate the baby. The hypothesis is that an agitated baby is a disturbed baby. The mother and her preborn baby become a hormonal communication unit: When mother is upset, baby is upset. Constant exposure of the baby's developing brain to stress hormones may result in an overcharged nervous system, resulting in a fussy baby.

Here's how you bond with your preborn baby and create a peaceful womb experience:

1. Resolve stress promptly. Most mothers experience some stress during pregnancy because of their normal ambivalent feelings and because changes happen so fast. How quickly and effectively you deal with this stress is important. Researchers in fetal awareness believe that temporary stresses do not have any lasting ef-

fects on the fetus. Chronic, unresolved conflicts and anxiety throughout most of the final months of pregnancy are most likely to disturb the baby, who may share your emotions.

2. Talk and sing to your baby. Give your baby pleasant womb memories. Studies have shown that infants later react to the famliar voices that talked and sang to them in utero. Newborns were better able to attend to their fathers' voices if they had talked to them before birth, and children were able to learn more easily those songs that their mothers had sung to them in the womb.

3. Play harmonious, calming music. Preborn babies are calmed by soothing music such as Vivaldi, Mozart, and classical guitar, but they are agitated by rock music. Professional musicians claim they were able to learn more easily the musical instruments their mothers played during pregnancy.

A custom that my wife and I have enjoyed during our pregnancies is talking to our baby each night before going to bed. This is especially important to get fathers hooked on their babies before birth. Each night I laid my hands on the "bulge," as we affectionately called this person, and I talked to our baby. After our son's birth, I was so accustomed to this practice I couldn't get to sleep unless I first went over and put my hands on his head and talked to this little person that I had gotten to know while he was still inside.

A valuable reference book for advice on bonding with your preborn baby and developing a deeper understanding of fetal awareness is *The Secret Life of the Unborn Child,* by Dr. Thomas Verny and John Kelly (Summit Books, 1981).

5

~~~~~~

MOTHERING YOUR PREBORN CHILD

Consider your baby a part of your body. What goes into you goes into your baby. Above all, *avoid smoking.* Nicotine decreases the blood supply to the placenta and therefore to your baby. Smoking increases the risk of prematurity, lowers the baby's weight, and slows brain growth. These effects increase in proportion to the number of cigarettes you smoke daily.

Drink alcohol with great caution during pregnancy. Fortunately, most mothers develop a natural aversion to alcohol during pregnancy. Drinking during pregnancy can cause fetal alcohol syndrome (FAS), manifested by unusual facial features, diminished growth, and, in severe cases, mental retardation. The amount of alcohol you can safely drink without damaging your preborn baby is unknown; we do know that five or more drinks on one occasion (binge drinking) or an average of two drinks per day throughout pregnancy can harm the fetus. (The term "drink" is defined as one ounce of alcohol, one twelve-ounce glass of beer, or one eight-ounce glass of wine.) Both the American Academy of Pediatrics and the American College of Obstetrics and Gynecology recommend abstaining from alcohol during pregnancy.

Medications during pregnancy. Be sure to check with your doctor before taking even over-the-counter drugs. Most drugs cross the placenta and may enter your preborn baby. While there are only a handful of drugs that are proven to harm the fetus, our knowledge of the effects of drugs during pregnancy is incomplete. Smoking, alcohol, and drugs have a "threshold effect," meaning that a lot of the substance may harm the fetus a lot, a little may harm the fetus a little, and very small amounts may not harm the fetus at all.

Avoid drugs such as cocaine, heroin, and marijuana during pregnancy.

Eat right during your pregnancy. Feeding your baby begins before birth. Good prenatal nutrition, or the lack of it, can affect the development of your preborn baby. Until recent years, not looking pregnant was the fashion, and doctors put limits on weight gain during pregnancy. Now we know that it is normal and healthy for both mother and baby to gain significant weight during pregnancy. You should expect to gain between 22 and 27 pounds (10–12 kg), which is composed of the following:

- Weight of extra blood volume and body fluids—8½ lbs.
- Baby—7½ lbs.
- Uterus—3½ lbs.
- Amniotic fluid—2½ lbs.
- Placenta—1½ lbs.
- Breasts—1 lb.

A normal weight gain for most women is 3 pounds during the first trimester and an increase of 3½ pounds per month thereafter. Mothers who are underweight to begin with may show a larger weight gain during pregnancy. This is nature's message to you that you need more nutrition.

What you eat is more important than how much you eat. You require extra carbohydrates and healthy fats for the increased energy both you and your growing baby need. The increased tissues and blood require increased proteins, vitamins, and iron. Consider eating lots of the following foods during your pregnancy: fish, eggs, lean beef or chicken, liver, lots of fresh green leafy vegetables, dairy products (especially in the form of cheese and yogurt), whole grain cereals, yellow vegetables, fruits, and potatoes. It is unlikely you will put on excess weight by overindulging in them. Most excessive weight gain during pregnancy results from eating too much junk food. Avoid excess salt, crash diets, and restricted meals during pregnancy. Your diet and appetite should parallel your pregnancy. During the last three months of pregnancy you may consume an excess of 500 nutritious calories a day without abnormal weight gain.

Expect some unusual food craving during your pregnancy. During our seventh pregnancy my wife, Martha, often woke up around midnight craving zucchini. As I stood in my overcoat and pajamas at the checkout line at an all-night supermarket holding a large zucchini in one hand, the clerk exclaimed, "Your wife must be pregnant!" While you deserve to pamper yourself in healthy food cravings, it is not wise to overindulge non-nutritious cravings. If you are eating properly and feeling well and do not have excessive swelling, indicating abnormal water retention, you do not have to worry about your weight gain.

Taking off weight safely after baby's birth. Some new mothers are in a hurry to return to their pre-pregnancy weight. Remember, it took nine months to put it on; normally it takes nine months to take it off. Crash diets are unhealthy and unwise both during pregnancy and after birth, especially if you are breastfeeding. Take off your excess weight as you put it on, slowly and steady. Remember, it is normal to retain a lot of excess fat during the first year after birth. This is nature's way of ensuring extra energy reserves that mothers need to meet the nutritional and physical demands of a new baby. Exercise is the safest way to lose weight after birth because you burn off extra fat and do not deprive your body of valuable energy nutrients. In our practice, we advise mothers to follow two simple methods of weight reduction: Avoid overdosing on junk food (high-fat foods and heavily sugared foods), and maintain a steady diet of at least a half hour a day of sustained exercise, such as a brisk walk while carrying your baby. If practiced daily, this program should yield a weight loss of one pound per week—a safe, effective rate.

6

CHOOSING WHETHER TO BREASTFEED OR FORMULA-FEED

B ecause you will spend more time feeding your baby than in any other interaction during the early months, it is important to choose a style of feeding that you enjoy. Usually as the baby's birth nears, women make up their mind how to feed their baby. This section is written for mothers who are still undecided about which style of feeding to use.

If by the time your baby's birth is at hand you are still on the fence, consider trying the following: Attend a series of La Leche League meetings while still pregnant. Meet other breastfeeding mothers and ask them what breastfeeding has done for them and their baby. Talk to friends who used both methods—but remember this is a very individual decision involving individual preferences and lifestyles. It is important to surround yourself with likeminded supporting mothers because breastfeeding is a lifestyle, not just a method of feeding. Most women today are intellectually convinced that breastfeeding is best but are not emotionally prepared for the commitment this style of feeding takes. Don't be discouraged by wellmeaning friends who volunteer that "breastfeeding didn't work for me"—most of the time it didn't because they breastfed in a nonsupportive atmosphere and without professional help.

If by the time of your baby's birth you are still undecided, I suggest you try the following: Begin breastfeeding your baby, using the right-start tips discussed in Key 7. Give it a 30-day free trial. If by the end of this period it is working for you, then by all means continue. If you do not anticipate most feedings with joy, if you feel pressured to breastfeed and really do not wish to, then consider an alternative method of feeding, or a combination of both. Remember, it is important to feed your baby in a way that works for both of you.

Over the past 30 years, the incidence of breastfeeding has increased from a pitiful 20 percent to a nationwide incidence of 60 percent. In some areas the rate is as high as 90 percent. The advantages of breastfeeding are discussed in Barron's *Keys to Breastfeeding.*

7

^^

BREASTFEEDING— RIGHT-START TECHNIQUES

One of the most valuable changes that has taken place in parenting over the past several decades is the return to breastfeeding. My wife, Martha, a lactation consultant who runs The Breastfeeding Center in San Clemente, California, and I have surveyed the patients who have come through the center and found the right-start techniques that have worked best for them. These suggestions are meant not only to encourage you to breastfeed but to help you better enjoy your breastfeeding relationship.

1. **Prenatal preparation and education.** During your last trimester of pregnancy, attend a series of La Leche League meetings. There are La Leche League meetings in every city; for the name and address of your nearest group call 1-800-La-Leche. You will be exposed to one of the most time-honored educational systems: mothers teaching mothers. You will also make valuable acquaintances who can help you overcome breastfeeding difficulties after birth. Before the birth of your baby, read as much as you can about breastfeeding. Two suggested sources are Barron's *Keys to Breastfeeding* and *The Womanly Art of Breastfeeding*, published by La Leche League International.

2. **Room in with your baby after birth.** Mothers who room in get off to a better start breastfeeding their baby because they spend more time with their baby and are able to work out a feeding system that works for them over the first few days.

3. **Breastfeed on cue rather than on schedule.** Mothers who feed their newborns more frequently are more likely to have a more successful breastfeeding relationship. It is the frequency of breastfeeding rather than the duration of each feeding that best stimulates milk production. Cue-feeding mothers experience fewer breast infections, enjoy their breastfeeding experience more, and have their milk come in much sooner.

4. **Seek advice from a trained lactation consultant** during the first 48 hours after your baby's birth. Nearly all hospitals have on their obstetrical staff certified lactation consultants, mothers who have previously breastfed their own infants and have taken courses on how to help the new mother get the right start. Lactation consultants can show you how to properly position yourself and your baby during breastfeeding, how to encourage your baby to latch on properly, and how to avoid sore nipples and engorged breasts. In my practice, I have found that most mothers who do not enjoy their breastfeeding experience or those for whom it has not worked did not obtain expert advice soon enough or at all.

5. **Avoid the "busy nest."** Breastfeeding is a lifestyle, not just a method of delivering milk. One of the most common reasons for breastfeeding failures during the newborn period is that the

24

mother is too busy with activities that take her energy away from her mothering. In teaching breastfeeding classes, my wife tells her expectant mothers to devote themselves fully to mothering their babies and to delegate all household chores to other members of the family. Basically, the early weeks should be spent doing what no one else can do, mothering your baby.

6. **Sleep close to your baby.** During the early weeks babies do not sleep through the night. Experienced breastfeeding mothers have found that nighttime feeding is much easier if they shorten the distance between themselves and their baby. Keep your baby in close nursing distance to you so when your baby wakes up for feeding it becomes a relationship you enjoy and not a chore you resent. Eventually you will achieve nighttime feeding harmony in which you roll over and nurse your baby and neither member of the nursing pair completely awakens.

During the first months, feeding your baby will take up a great deal of your time. These right-start techniques are geared toward helping you enjoy breastfeeding your baby.

8

BONDING WITH YOUR
NEWBORN BABY

B onding is the term for the close physical and emotional attachment that develops between you and your baby at the time of birth. It is really a continuation of the bond that you began to form with your baby during your pregnancy, strengthened by your constant awareness of the life inside you. The physical and chemical changes occurring in your body remind you of the presence of this being. After birth, this bond does not stop simply because your baby is no longer a part of your body. Birth cements this bond and gives it reality. You now can see, feel, and talk to the little person whom you knew only by "the bulge," the movements, and the heartbeat you heard through medical instruments. Bonding allows you to transfer your life-giving love for the infant inside to the care-giving love for the one outside. Inside, you gave your blood; outside you give your milk, your eyes, your hands, your voice—your entire self. Unless a medical complication prevents it, this continuum should not be interrupted by trivial routines or diluted by depressing medications.

How does this early bonding affect you and your baby? Medical science is continually trying to prove what mothers have intuitively known—that something good happens to mothers and babies when they bond with each other at birth. Much of the research of mother-infant bonding was popularized by Drs. Klaus and Kennell in their book, *Parent-Infant*

Bonding, in which they compared two groups of mothering styles. The early-contact group bonded with their babies immediately after birth and the delayed-contact group was temporarily separated from their babies immediately after birth. They found that the following mothering abilities were greater in the early-contact group: They were more successful at breastfeeding, talked with their infants more and used more descriptive speech, spent more time in the face to face (enface) position of eye-to-eye contact, and touched and groomed their infants more.

These researchers concluded there is a sensitive period, lasting about one hour after birth, when the baby is most receptive to his caregiver. Mothers who bonded with their babies during this period were more confident in exercising their intuitive mothering, while mothers who were separated during this period were less confident. The researchers also found that fathers who were present at delivery and who bonded with their babies during this period continued this involvement and were closer to their children.

What about the newborn who for some reason, such as prematurity or caesarean delivery, is temporarily separated from his mother? What happens in the case of adoption? Is the parent-baby relationship permanently affected by the loss of very early contact, or can one make up for what the baby has missed? Recent studies have questioned the conclusion that bonding during the first hour after birth has any lasting effect on either parent or child. This is an important point: Parents who are unable to bond with their baby immediately after birth should not feel guilty because they fear their child has been permanently deprived. Immediate bonding after birth is not like instant glue that cements the parent-infant relationship forever. Many steps may be taken throughout infancy and childhood that lead to a strong parent-infant attachment. While there is probably no scientific rationale for concluding that being deprived of this initial bonding can permanently affect either parent or child, I believe that bonding during this biologically sensitive period gives the entire parent-infant relationship a head start. I suspect that as soon as mothers and babies are reunited, a strong mother-infant attachment can compensate for the loss of this early opportunity for bonding; I have seen adopting parents who, upon first contact with their one-week-old newborn, release feelings as deep and as caring as those of the biological parents in the delivery room.

If a mother is unable to hold her baby immediately after birth because of medical complications, I believe that a father should be invited to hold his baby in the delivery room and in the newborn nursery. Studies have shown that fathers of infants delivered by caesarean who are given a chance to hold the baby within minutes of the birth engaged in significantly more caregiving activities six months later, especially in relation to soothing the baby, than those fathers who did not get to greet their infants until several hours after birth.

How bonding occurs. Picture yourself in the delivery room at your baby's birth. Let's go through how I believe bonding should occur.

Ideally, unless prevented by a medical complication, immediately after delivery the infant should be placed skin-to-skin on the mother's abdomen, baby's head nestling between her breasts, with the baby's back and head covered with a warm towel. (This is not just good psychology; it is good medicine, because newborns easily get cold.) Imagine what a warm, snugly place this first new home is. Draping a baby over mother, tummy to tummy, cheek to breast, allows a natural heat transfer from the mother to the infant. The first hour after birth is prime time for receptivity for mother and infant—a sensitive period in which both mother and newborn are programmed to recognize and get to know each other.

Within minutes after birth, the newborn enters the state of quiet alertness in which baby is most able to take from and give to the environment. During this alert stage the baby looks directly at the mother's eyes and snuggles at her breasts, both sharing a mutual need, the baby's need to be held and comforted and a mother's need to be with her baby. Do not be surprised if during this first meeting your newborn seems to be relatively still, almost as if he is so enthralled with what he sees, hears, and feels that he doesn't want to waste any energy squirming. During this early bonding, your baby drinks in the sound of your voice, the feel of your warm skin, and the taste of your breasts. Within minutes after birth, the infant begins to feel to whom he belongs. As baby continues to nurse, mother continues to soothe. Both feel "right." Within an hour or two after the birth, the baby contently drifts into a deep sleep.

Imagine for a moment just what your baby learns during this first meeting. He learns a very important fact about his new world: distress is followed by comfort. In so doing he learns the single most valuable lesson in infant development—that he can trust his environment.

Within minutes after birth, the physical bonding between parents and baby is extended to emotional bonding. I have noticed that in the first meeting mothers and fathers look at their newborn with a sort of wide-angle lens, getting an overall picture of the uniqueness of this new little person. Then they gradually focus on their newborn's specific characteristics. New parents immediately see their newborn as a person, a new member of the family. "He has your ears," mother may say to father. "She has her grandmother's nose," parents may exclaim. Even in the first few minutes after birth you begin to notice patterns of behavior in your baby, such as sucking his thumb or having his hands in constant contact with your face, patterns that must have begun in the womb. You smile at feeling those very same movements of little feet and knees, recognizing the familiar rhythm and intensity that you felt while baby was inside.

The following suggestions are designed to help you get off to a good start and help make your bonding relationship a more meaningful experience.

1. A positive birthing experience usually encourages maternal bonding, while a negative birthing experience dominated by fear and pain often lessens the mother's desire to bond with her infant. Three important factors contribute to a positive birthing experience and therefore promote a positive bonding experience: a good prepared childbirth class, a trained labor support person, and the right birthing environment (see Keys 1 and 2).

2. Private time should be respected. After the delivery room personnel have attended to mother and baby and if both are well, you should request some private time alone for just the three of you—mother, father, and baby. This is a special time of family intimacy that should not be interrupted.

3. Breastfeed your baby right after delivery. Some babies have a strong desire to suckle the breast immediately after birth, and others are content simply to lick the nipple. Medical research clearly demonstrates that babies should be put

to the breast immediately after birth. Sucking and licking the nipple release the hormone oxytocin, which increases the contractions of your uterus and lessens the complications of postpartum bleeding, into your blood stream and stimulates the release of the hormone prolactin, the hormone that enhances your mothering abilities right from the start.

4. Touch your baby. As we have said, ideally, immediately after birth your baby should be dried off and placed nude on you, his chest to your abdomen, with your arms around him and a blanket over your arms. Your newborn will enjoy the stimulation that he receives from his skin-to-skin contact. Gently stroke your new baby, touching his whole body. It is moving to see a new mother stroke her baby's entire body with a gentle caress of her fingertips and to see the father place an entire hand on his baby's head as if symbolizing his commitment to protect the life he has fathered. Besides, stroking has medical benefits. The skin is the largest organ in the human body and is very rich with nerve endings. At a crucial transition into baby's entry into the world, when breathing patterns are often very irregular, stroking stimulates the newborn to breath more rhythmically. Your touch has therapeutic value.

5. Gaze at your baby. Place your baby in the enface position so that your eyes and your baby's eyes meet on the same vertical plane. Your newborn can see you best within a distance of 12 inches. Because they are in a state of quiet alertness after birth, many infants open their eyes more during the first hour after birth than they will several

hours after birth when they are usually asleep. Staring into your baby's eyes may trigger a rash of beautiful mothering feelings. Ask the nurses to delay putting ointment in your baby's eyes until after the bonding period since it may blur baby's vision at the very time she is developing her first impression of you.

6. Talk to your newborn. Mothers naturally speak to their newborns in high-pitched, comforting voices. Your baby's ears are already attuned to your speech, and you may notice that she moves rhythmically in response to your voice.

Holding, nursing, talking to, and staring into your baby's eyes may make you feel you don't want to release this little person that you have labored so hard to bring into the world— and you don't have to!

9

ROOMING IN WITH YOUR NEWBORN

Bonding does not end in the delivery room; it begins there. To further enhance it, healthy mothers and babies should be together until they are discharged from the hospital.

The advantages of rooming in Rooming-in is the natural extension of the birth-bonding period. After birth both you and your baby may fall into a much-deserved sleep. After the baby's initial hour of alertness, she will probably reward you by sleeping for two or three hours. For most mothers, the ecstasy of birth is eventually overruled by exhaustion.

The next attachment decision is to select your baby's primary caregiver in the hospital—you or the nursery staff. There are many options for newborn care, some of which unfortunately may interfere with mother-infant attachment in the hospital. One option, which I strongly discourage, is giving the baby's primary care to the nursery staff, who bring the baby to the mother on a predetermined schedule or at their convenience. In my opinion, this option should be reserved only for sick mothers with sick babies. Not only does it deprive the mother of caring for the life she nourished for so long, but, I sincerely feel, it is not in the best interests of the mother or infant. Scheduled newborn care puts the mother in the role of secondary caregiver, an unbecoming role. Hospitals should not consider mothering a drug for the baby, dispensed in concentrated doses at prescribed times.

The second option, and the one that many mothers elect, is that of modified rooming-in, in which the newborn spends most of the day with the mother but spends the night in the nursery and is brought out on demand for night feedings. In theory this modified type of rooming-in seems attractive. Actually, this situation often become confusing to both mother and baby, and the baby may wind up spending a lot of the time in the nursery.

The third option, and the one I strongly encourage, is full rooming-in. Full rooming-in allows you to exercise your mothering instincts immediately, when the hormones in your body are programmed for it. Studies have shown that infants who room in with their mothers cry less and more readily organize their sleep-wake cycles. The mother and the baby who fully room enjoy the following benefits:

- The mother has fewer breastfeeding problems. Her milk comes in sooner, and her infant is more satisfied.
- The infant has less jaundice, probably because she gets more milk.
- The mother actually seems to get more rest, since she experiences less separation anxiety and the newborn sleeps most of the time anyway. (A new mother may erroneously be led to believe that she will rest better if her baby is in the nursery. In reality, this is seldom true.)
- Babies in a large nursery are soothed by tape recordings of a human heartbeat or music. Rather than being soothed electronically, the baby who is rooming with his mother is soothed by the real thing.
- The newborn seems more content because he interacts with only one caregiver, his mother. Hospital personnel can focus their attention and care on the mother, who is then more comfortable and able to focus her care on her baby. The rooming-in mother is much more competent and intuitive in the care of her newborn when they go home.

• The rooming-in mother has a lower incidence of postpartum depression.

Attachment-promoting behaviors Every new mother wonders, "How will I ever take care of this little person? Will I be a good mother?" The intense desire to be a good mother, coupled with your intense love for your newborn, is likely to bring out normal feelings of doubt; the system of mother-newborn care will work as long as the conditions are right. I believe that every mother is perfectly capable of nurturing her child and that every tiny newborn has a signaling system that will tell the mother what he needs.

All babies are born with a group of special qualities called, in child-development jargon, *attachment-promoting behaviors*—features and behaviors designed to alert the caregiver to the baby's presence and draw the caregiver, magnetlike, toward the baby. These features are the roundness of baby's eyes, cheeks, and body; the softness of baby's skin; the relative bigness of the baby's eyes; and, perhaps the most important of all, baby's early language—his cries and pre-crying noises.

A baby's cry is designed to promote her survival and the development of the mother instinct. The opening sounds of the baby's cry activate or release the mother's physical and emotional feelings. Upon hearing her baby cry, the mother experiences an increased flow of blood to her breasts, and she has the biological urge to pick up and nurse her baby. This is one of the strongest examples of the biological signals of the baby triggering a biological response in the mother. There is no other signal in the world that triggers such intense emotions in a mother as her baby's cry; at no other time in a child's life will the language of the child so forcefully stimulate the mother to act.

Picture what happens when babies and mothers room in together. Baby begins to cry. Mother, because she is there and attuned to her baby, immediately picks up and nurses the baby. Baby stops crying. The next time baby awakens, squirms, grimaces, and then cries, mother responds in the same manner. The next time, mother notices her baby's pre-crying cues. When baby awakens, squirms, and grimaces, mother picks up and nurses baby *before* he has to cry. Mother has learned her baby's signals and responds appropriately. After rehearsing this dialogue many times during the rooming-in period, mother and baby work as a team. Baby learns to cue better, and mother learns to respond better. After a couple days of this stimulus-response activity, mother begins to notice amazing biological changes triggered by her baby's cry. In response to her baby's cry and appearance and the feel of her baby, her breasts begin to feel full and she has the sensation of milk letting down from the back part of her breasts to the front. The attachment-promoting cries elicit this hormonal response in the mother; the mother and infant are in biological harmony.

Contrast this rooming-in scene with that of an infant cared for in a hospital nursery. The newborn infant, lying in a plastic box, awakens hungry, and cries, along with 20 other babies in plastic boxes who have by now all managed to awaken each other. A kind and caring nurse, but an individual with no biological attachment to the baby, hears the cries and responds as soon as time permits. The crying, hungry baby is taken to his mother in due time. The problem is that a baby's cry has two phases: The early sounds of a baby's cries have an attachment promoting quality, while the sounds of an unattended cry are more disturbing to listen to and actually promote avoidance.

The mother, who has missed out on this biological drama, is nonetheless expected to give a nurturing response to her baby some minutes later. By this time the infant has either retreated into a deep sleep or is now greeting the mother with intense, upsetting wails. The mother, who possesses the biological attachment to the baby, nevertheless hears only the cries that are more likely to elicit an agitated concern rather than tenderness. Even though she has a comforting breast to offer the baby, she may be so tied up in knots that her milk won't let down, and the baby cries even harder. As she grows to doubt her ability to comfort her baby, the infant may wind up spending *more* time in the nursery. This separation leads to more missed cues, more breaks in the attachment between mother and baby, and they leave the hospital together more or less strangers.

When I was in charge of a newborn nursery, we coined the phrase, "Nursery-reared babies learn to cry harder; rooming-in babies learn to cry better." Rooming in truly does allow the best of both worlds; in my opinion, it is ideal.

10

‸‸

WHAT NEWBORNS LOOK LIKE

As soon as your baby is handed to you after birth, you will immediately notice that she does not look like baby-book pictures. Some writers have unfeelingly described the newborn baby as looking like a prize fighter, although I have never heard a mother say this. Despite all the physical evidence that the baby has worked hard coming through the birth canal, you will find him beautiful.

Baby will show signs of having had to squeeze a bit to enter the world. His red face may have areas of blueish purple and may be dotted with freckled spots caused by tiny broken blood vessels. The fluid that accumulates beneath the skin causes a puffy face and eyelids; in fact, you may not get a complete look at your baby's eyes for several days. Because of the baby's tight squeeze through the birth canal, he may have a flattened nose, ears pressed against his head, and a slight bruising of the skin over the prominent cheekbones.

Your baby's head may have the shape of a watermelon. This shape, the result of a process called molding, is necessary to help your baby's head fit through the pelvic bones during delivery, and protects the underlying brain. The top of your baby's skull is made up of many bones joined together by tough membranes. As your baby's head enters the birth canal, these bones move and allow the head to elongate to conform more easily to the changing shape of the birth canal. You may feel ridges on the top of your baby's head that are caused by the overlapping of these bones. Molding is more noticeable after long labors and in babies with larger heads; it is less noticeable in breech presentations and may not be present at all in babies delivered by caesarean. In any event, your baby's head will assume a more rounded shape within a few days.

As you examine your baby's head, you will notice a relatively soft area in the center top of the newborn's head where the skull bones join. This soft spot, called a fontanelle, is covered by a thick membrane. It will gradually get smaller as the bones in your baby's skull grow together. There is another smaller fontanelle in the center of the back of your baby's head. It's okay to touch and wash these soft spots; actually they are very tough. Sometimes you'll be able to see and feel a pulse through the soft spot.

Your baby's scalp is usually very swollen because of the squeeze through the birth canal. This swelling, called a caput, usually disappears along with the molding a few days after birth. Sometimes, tiny blood vessels beneath the scalp break during delivery, allowing blood to accumulate and form a sort of "goose egg" on baby's scalp. This may take several months to disappear and sometimes may feel very hard as the underlying blood calcifies.

Your newborn's skin is covered with a white, cheesy, slippery material called vernix. This protects the skin from the amniotic fluid and acts like a lubricant during delivery. The vernix, specks of blood, and amniotic fluid are matted in your baby's fine silky hair. Along your baby's back, earlobes, cheeks and shoulders there are patches of fine furry hair called lanugo. This early baby hair disappears in a few months. Skin looks and feels different from baby to baby; some babies have smooth, tight-fitting skin, while others (especially postmature or small-for-date babies) have loose-fitting, wrinkled skin. It is normal for baby's skin to be dry, flaky, and cracked, especially on the hands and feet. It is also normal for your baby's hands and feet to remain blue for several hours after birth and periodically during the first week. You may notice any of a number of common birthmarks and skin discolorations, which are described in Key 28.

Newborn babies have large fatty areas, called fat folds, along the back of the neck, the cheeks, the sides of the nose, and underneath the arms. Most babies have fat folds that cause double chins, making it very hard to see baby's short neck.

Baby's eyes are the most fascinating part of your newborn's face. The puffy eyelids with the slit-like openings protect the newborn's sensitive eyes from too much light too soon. Newborns seldom keep their eyes wide open for very long. They have intermittent periods of visual alertness after which they drift off into stages of deepening sleep. It is normal for one or both eyelids to droop temporarily for a few days or weeks before baby's eyes are completely wide open. It is also normal to have a tiny broken blood vessel in the white part of the eyes. This clears within a few weeks. (See Key 18 for a description of what a newborn can see.)

During the first few days, your newborn will lie in a position similar to the ones he was accustomed to in your womb. The arms and legs flex toward the body in a frog-like position. The hands are drawn up toward the face and some newborns even begin caressing their faces within the first few hours after birth. A newborn's fists are tightly clenched most of the time, and her bowed legs and turned-in feet are pulled up beneath her.

Enjoy how your newborn looks and acts because next month these beautiful characteristics will change.

11

^^

NEWBORN REFLEXES

B abies are capable of two kinds of actions: cognitive and reflexive. Cognitive acts are those that baby thinks about and decides on before acting. For example, when a baby is shown a rattle, the thinking part of her brain decides, "I'll use my hand to get the rattle"; the brain then sends a message to the muscles, instructing them to grab the rattle. Reflexive actions, on the other hand, are automatic. A familiar example is the knee-jerk reflex. When your knee is tapped at just the right place, you don't think, "Now I must extend my leg"; your leg extends automatically. Much of a newborn baby's movement is reflexive, and many of these reflexes are self-protective. Newborns exhibit about 70 primitive reflexes; some of the most common and interesting, especially those that have survival benefits, are described in this key.

Sucking and swallowing is the most important survival reflex. Babies automatically suck in response to stimulation of (in decreasing levels of sensitivity) the soft palate, the interior of the mouth and lips, and the cheek and chin. These reflexes are most easily elicited close to baby's feeding time.

Tied in with the sucking reflex is the **rooting** or **search reflex.** When mother's nipple tickles baby's face, baby will search or root for the nipple by turning her head and mouth. This reflex helps baby find the nipple more easily. I believe that the rooting reflex is important to nighttime nursing; the baby sleeps nestled up against mother's breasts, and baby's reflexes help her zero in on the nipple and help herself to a nighttime feeding. In our family we call this nighttime feeding "self-serve," as opposed to "full-serve" of the usual daytime nursing. Both these reflexes, also called mouthing reflexes, enable babies to find a source of food. Don't tickle baby's cheek to encourage her to breastfeed; this causes her to turn her head out of alignment, perhaps interfering with normal sucking and swallowing. It is better to turn the whole baby on her side to face your breast, her tummy to your tummy, and stimulate your baby to open her mouth by brushing her lips with your nipple.

The Moro reflex (startle response) occurs in response to a sudden, disturbing noise or a sudden withdrawal of support to a baby's head and neck. In reaction to this sensation of falling, baby quickly extends her arms out from her body as if trying to cling to and embrace someone and then brings them in. This reflex is accompanied by grimacing or crying, especially if there is no one to grab onto for comfort. This clinging response is a protective reflex; baby needs a person between those embracing little arms. This reflex gradually lessens and disappears by three to six months.

The grasp reflex is another protective reflex. It allows a baby to hold an object with her hands. If you stimulate the palm of your baby's hands with your finger by placing your finger into her palm from the side of the hand opposite the thumb, her fingers will wrap tenaciously around yours. If you begin to lift your baby by your finger, you will notice that her arms and wrist muscles tense as she is helping to pull herself up. Her grasp intensifies and has such strength that you can actually lift baby partially off the surface she is lying on before she lets go. A similar reflex can be elicited by gently stroking the soles of your baby's feet behind the toes; her toes will grab your finger. The grasp reflex usually disappears by the third month. Anthropologists have speculated that the moro reflex and the grasp reflex are remnants of attachment behaviors used by human infants to hold onto their mothers as other primates do.

The fencer's reflex (also called tonic neck reflex) encourages baby to look at the hand extended in front of her face. If you turn your baby's head to one side while she is lying on her back, her arm and leg on that side will thrust outward while the opposite arm and leg flex, resembling the *en garde* position of a fencer. In some ways this reflex inhibits baby from using her arms, hands, and head in midline play—that is, in front of her body. The tonic neck reflex subsides at around three to four months, allowing the infant to engage in stimulating hand-eye play.

The withdrawal reflex is often noticed in newborns during a blood test. If a painful stimulus is given to the foot of the baby (such as pricking the heel to obtain blood), the leg and foot flex in withdrawal to avoid the pain. At the same time, the other leg thrusts outward as if to push the painful stimulus away.

Righting reflexes, which help the baby learn to keep her head, trunk, arms, and legs in proper alignment for survival and motor development, mature during the first year of life. The most obvious righting reflex in the newborn period is baby's attempt to keep her head where it ought to be in relation to the rest of her body. If you place your baby face down, she will momentarily lift her head just enough to clear the surface and turn it to one side. If you pull your baby up by her hands to a sitting position, she will tense and elevate her shoulders in an attempt to keep her large head from wobbling from side to side or overshooting the mark and falling forward.

The stepping reflex is interesting and fun to test on your newborn. Hold your baby upright over a table so that the sole of one foot presses on the table. The weight-bearing foot will lift up while the other foot will lower as if baby is beginning to take a step. This reflex usually disappears in the second month.

Another interesting protective reflex might be called the **smothering avoidance reflex.** If a light blanket is placed over baby's nose and mouth, she will mouth it initially and then twist her head vigorously from side to side or cross each arm over her face in an attempt to knock the blanket off.

The gag reflex begins in the newborn period and persists throughout life. Stimulation of the back of the throat causes the jaw to lower and the tongue to thrust forward and downward. This automatically expels an object from baby's throat, protecting her from choking while she learns to feed and swallow.

Your baby's reflexes are more than just curiosities. They are necessary to survival and development. Watching them enhances your appreciation of this little person's amazing capabilities.

12

‸‸

ROUTINE TESTS, INJECTIONS AND MEDICATIONS

A number of tests are done on all newborns to detect quickly any possible medical conditions that may require treatment. In addition, babies receive a number of preventive injections and medications. This key describes some of the most common tests and medications given routinely to newborns.

The Apgar score. This test was formulated by Dr. Virginia Apgar to assess the health of the baby within the first five minutes after birth and to help medical personnel assess which type of medical care a newborn baby might need. A baby with a low score was put in a nursery to be watched more carefully and to receive more skilled nursing care; babies with a higher score did not need to be put in a special nursery. The Apgar evaluation is performed at one and five minutes after birth. The newborn is given from 0 to 2 points for each of the following parameters: color, breathing efforts, heart rate, muscle tone, and general reflexes. An infant who receives a score of 10 has received 2 points for each of these parameters, indicating that each system is functioning at its maximum; a score at the lower end of the scale (4 or 5) indicate that some of these systems are not functioning at their best within the first five minutes after birth.

Although infants who are pink all over, cry lustily, breathe rapidly, have rapid heart rates, and show strong muscle movements are usually given scores of 10, most normal, healthy newborns do not achieve perfect scores. It is quite normal for a newborn baby to have blue hands and feet because it takes a few minutes for the newborn's circulatory system to become adjusted to the postnatal environment. For this the baby loses a point. Also, some babies are naturally quiet immediately after birth and therefore lose points for not crying lustily. The state of quiet alertness is more desirable than crying even though the baby who does not cry may receive a lower Apgar score. Medically speaking, parents need not be given this score because a low score may become a source of unnecessary anxiety. But since most parents ask, it is important to know the real meaning of this score. If your baby has pink lips and skin and is breathing normally, chances are he is very healthy at birth.

Eye ointment. Erythromycin, an antibiotic, is put into your baby's eyes to protect against germs that may have entered the eyes during passage through the birth canal. This ointment will in no way harm your baby's eyes. Because it is important for your baby to gaze into your eyes immediately after birth—one of the high points of bonding—you may safely request the nurse to delay administering this eye care for an hour or two after birth.

Blood tests. Within the first few days after birth a few drops of your baby's blood is taken to test for several illnesses. **Phenylketonuria (PKU)** is an extremely rare disease, occurring in approximately one out of 15,000 infants, that, left untreated, can result in brain damage; if detected early and treated properly, the child may develop normally. Your baby's blood is also tested for **hypothyroidism,** a condition, occurring in one out of every 5,000 infants, caused by a sluggish thyroid. If left untreated, hypothyroidism may cause mental retardation; the earlier it is detected, the more effective is the treatment. Another infection detected by this blood test is **galactosemia,** occurring in one out of every 60,000 infants. It is caused by an enzyme deficiency that allows harmful substances to build up in a baby's blood and cause tissue damage. Like **PKU,** this disease is treatable by a special diet. It is important for parents to realize that these illnesses, though rare, are treatable, but if the tests are omitted and the diagnosis and treatment delayed, some vital organs may be damaged. Most states have laws requiring these tests to be done in the newborn period.

Vitamin K. An injection of Vitamin K is given to your newborn immediately after birth. Vitamin K, in which many newborns are deficient, promotes normal blood clotting. This injection lessens the risk of abnormal bleeding into vital tissues. Like the eye ointment, this injection can be delayed for a few hours until after parents and baby have bonded.

Newborn jaundice. Although extremely common, newborn jaundice is frequently a source of anxiety to parents. In reality, it is a variant of a normal physiologic process.

Newborns may develop two types of jaundice: normal and abnormal. Many babies develop the normal type, also called physiologic jaundice, around three to four days after birth. It is the result of immaturity of the liver. Most babies are born with more blood cells than they need; normally the excess red blood cells are broken down, releasing bilirubin (a yellow pigment). Because the newborn liver is immature, it is unable to process the excess bilirubin, which is then deposited in the skin, giving your baby a yellow color. This type of jaundice, which gradually disappears by a week or two, does not harm your baby and, according to the most recent medical knowledge, does not cause brain damage.

47

Abnormal jaundice may be caused either by a difference in blood group (Rh factor) between mother and child or by an infection in the newborn. In one type of abnormal type of jaundice, the bilirubin levels may go high enough to cause brain damage. The cause of this jaundice is usually blood group incompatibility. Even this type of jaundice is seldom a problem except in premature or sick babies. Your doctor will inform you which type of jaundice your baby has and whether you need to be concerned. If your baby has a high level of abnormal jaundice, the most common treatment is phototherapy, in which your baby is placed under a fluorescent light that dissolves the bilirubin the skin, allowing it to be disposed of more adequately through the kidneys. Sometimes jaundice can be aggravated if the baby does not get enough to eat and gets dehydrated. If your baby has jaundice, be sure to ask your doctor the nature of the problem. In my experience, too much parental anxiety is attached to this normal physiologic process at a time when parents are particularly vulnerable to any suggestion that something may be wrong with their baby.

13

~~~~~~

EARLY NEWBORN CHANGES

One of the most exciting aspects of parenting is seeing how fast your newborn changes. The most notable changes occur in breathing patterns, bowel movements, and weight.

Newborn breathing patterns. If you watch your sleeping baby breathe, you will notice an irregular pattern. She appears to stop breathing periodically, sometimes for as long as ten to fifteen seconds, and then starts again without any apparent problem. This is called periodic breathing and is normal for the tiny baby. The younger or the more premature the baby, the more irregular the breathing pattern and the more noticeable the periodic breathing. Over the next few months, babies' breathing patterns become much more regular, although they continue to breathe much faster than adults. Sometimes near the end of a breath, a newborn may take a deep breath, a type of sigh, and then begin periodic breathing again.

In addition to being irregular breathers, newborns are noisy breathers. They accumulate a lot of mucus or saliva in the back of their throats, which causes a gurgly sound. Newborns are obligate nose breathers, which means that they breathe through their noses much more easily than through their mouths. Because their nasal passages are narrow, even a slight amount of congestion can result in noisy breathing. Babies seldom breathe with their mouths open. Even when

49

her mouth is open during sleep, a baby's tongue is curled up to the roof of her mouth, making it difficult for her to breathe through her mouth. Babies breathe better when placed on their stomachs with their heads turned slightly to one side, allowing the tongue and any mucus on the throat to come forward and making more room for air to pass.

Changes in your baby's excretion. In the first few days, babies' stools contain a black, tar-like, sticky substance called meconium, which is composed of amniotic fluid debris from the intestines. Over the next few days, the stools become less sticky and turn greenish-brown. Between one and two weeks they take on a yellowish color and a more regular consistency. Stools of breastfeeding babies are yellow and seedy, with a consistency like mustard and a not unpleasant buttermilk odor. The changes in a breastfed baby's stools give a clue to the changes in mother's milk; as the milk comes in and the amount of fat in it increases, the stools become more yellow and mustardlike. Because breast milk has a natural laxative effect, the stools of breastfed babies are more frequent and softer than the stools of formula-fed babies, which tend to be firmer and darker with an unpleasant odor. Added iron in the formula makes the stools greenish. The numbers of stools varies greatly in newborns. Some babies have a loose stool after every breastfeeding. A newborn who is getting a sufficient amount of breast milk usually has two to five bowel movements a day. Mothers often hear the gurgly sounds of a soft stool a few minutes into the feeding. While the stools of a newborn baby are usually mustard-yellow, an occasional green stool is of no consequence if baby seems generally well. Occasionally some babies have a hard stool or a sudden explosive stool that causes a tiny tear in baby's rectum, called a rectal fissure. This results in a few spots of bright red blood on baby's diaper or streaks of blood in his stools. Fissures usually heal easily; lubricating baby's rectum with pediatric glycerine suppositories, as advised by your doctor, can help.

The urine of newborn babies is very unconcentrated and water-like. After a few weeks it may take on a more concentrated yellow-amber color. It is common for newborns to have only two to three wet diapers during the first few weeks. Thereafter, a newborn should wet at least six to eight cloth diapers (four to five disposable) each day.

Newborn puberty. During the first week or two excess maternal hormones that cross the placenta into the baby's bloodstream during pregnancy may give rise to changes resembling the onset of puberty. Around the second or third week or sooner, you may notice that the baby's breasts are enlarged (in both male and female babies) and may even be secreting a few drops of milk. This is a normal response and will subside within a few weeks. Sometimes a newborn girl has a few drops of blood coming from the vagina that resemble a menstrual period. This is also normal. Most babies experience an acne-like rash on the face that appears around two weeks of age and disappears around six weeks.

Weight changes. Newborns usually lose five to eight percent of their birth weight (six to ten ounces) during the first week. Babies are born with extra fluid and fat to tide them over until their mother's milk can supply sufficient fluid and nutrition. Several factors affect the amount of weight a baby loses. Large babies who have a lot of extra fluid tend to lose more weight. Their skin may feel more wrinkled as they lose this extra fluid during the first week. Babies who room in with their mothers and are breastfed on cue tend to lose the least weight, if any at all. Babies born at home usually lose less weight than babies born in the hospital, not because of the location of the baby's birth but because home-birth and rooming-in babies are not separated from their mothers and therefore tend to nurse more often. Another factor influencing the amount of weight lost during the first week is how quickly the mother's milk comes in. Babies who are with their mothers constantly and can breastfeed frequently tend to lose less weight because the milk comes in sooner, giving them a higher-calorie milk as well as more of it. Babies who are separated from their mothers a lot during the first week or who are fed according to schedule tend to lose the most weight. In addition to recording baby's birth weight, parents should remember to record baby's weight upon discharge from the hospital; it is an important reference for measuring weight gain at the first check-up two or three weeks later. Breastfed babies usually show a slower weight gain than formula-fed babies during the first two weeks. Thereafter, breastfed babies and bottle fed babies show similar weight gains, averaging around an ounce a day during the last two weeks of the first month. Most babies gain an average of a pound to a pound and a half during the first month.

Another factor influencing your baby's weight gain is her body type. Ectomorph babies, recognized by their lean and lanky appearance, long fingers, and long, narrow feet, show a slower gain in weight and proportionately greater increase in height than do babies who are mesomorphs (medium build) or endomorphs (short, pudgy hands and feet and shorter, wider fingers and toes).

Newborn smiles. Perhaps the most enjoyable change during the first month is how your baby's smile changes between birth and the fourth week. For years parents and professionals have debated the subject of just how early babies smile and whether the smile indicates pleasure or gas. After 23 years of watching our own seven children and thousands of other newborns, I have concluded that newborns truly do smile, even on the first day. I divide baby's smiles into two types: inside smiles and outside smiles. In the first few weeks, baby's smiles—inside smiles—are a beautiful reflection of an inner feeling of rightness. These smiles, called sleep grins, usually occur while the baby is drifting off to sleep. They come in many forms; some are one-sided, some two-sided, some last for several seconds, some are fleeting. Inside smiles are often accompanied by other signs of relaxation: Baby goes totally limp and his arms dangle at his side, seemingly weightless. Newborns often smile immediately after release of tension or after they burp or pass gas. Baby's early smiles convey an "I feel good inside" message.

Occasionally, during the first month, some outside stimulus such as your own smiling or your facial expression may produce a smile on your baby's face. This outside, or social smiling, usually does not begin to any great degree until the second month. These smiles, when they appear, are a powerful enforcer of caregiver activity. You may become totally entranced by your newborn's smile. When you feel that his smiles arise from a feeling of goodness and rightness deep inside, you may feel ecstatic and feel good yourself. When you and your newborn begin to smile in sync with each other, you may feel completely at one with your baby, almost as though you are sharing a secret for which neither of you really knows the words but both know the feelings.

Newborn movements. Developing an appreciation for how your newborn uses his whole body sharpens your observation skills and helps you notice the subtle changes from month to month. Watching how your baby moves is one of the hallmarks of enjoying your baby.

When quiet or sleeping, newborn babies resume the fetal position, the position they grew accustomed to in utero. When lying on their tummies their legs are flexed up toward their abdomens and their feet are curled underneath the diaper area. Their bottoms are higher off the mattress than their heads. They can lift their heads and turn them just enough to make their noses clear the surface so they can breathe. Even as newborns, babies occasionally thrust out their legs as if trying to push off. When a newborn baby lies on his back, all his limbs are drawn in toward his body. His feet usually cross or touch each other.

You will notice that your newborn holds his hands close to his face most of the time. Periodically he rests his open hands on his face as if to stroke it; this is probably reminiscent of his actions in utero. Baby's fists are clenched, except when he is very relaxed or sleeping, at which time his fingers relax a bit and his hands open.

When playing with your newborn you will notice that his muscles have a spring-like feel. When you pull his arms or legs away from his body or try to open his hands, they quickly spring back to their original flexed position. As the weeks go by, you will notice baby's muscle tone become increasingly relaxed.

Baby's movements vary dramatically when he is lying on his back in the state of quiet alertness. He may rapidly thrust his arms and legs outward for no reason and then slowly return them to his torso. When startled, he may flail his limbs about in a jerky rhythm. Even when sleeping and apparently not upset, a newborn occasionally twitches and startles. The jerkiness of movements is especially prevalent in premature infants. These early muscle twitches are normal. Muscle twitches are especially common when the baby is passing from one stage of sleep to another. Newborn babies also move their arms and legs in smooth, rhythmic, freely-cycling movements resembling the action of a slow-motion movie. If you place your hands over baby's knee and elbow joints, you will often hear and feel clicking or crackling sounds. These are normal joint noises caused by the rubber-like ligaments and loose bones.

14

‸‸

NEST IN WITH
YOUR BABY

The bonding you enjoyed during the rooming-in with your baby in the hospital should continue over the next few weeks, the time I call the fitting-in period. It is a time for a nesting in, for mother and baby to refine their mutual attachment. Here are some tips to help you and your baby get the most out of this fitting-in period:

• **Define priorities.** My wife, Martha, advises the mothers in her childbirth classes, "Don't take your nightgown off for two weeks. Sit in your rocking chair and let yourself be mothered!" Here is what we humorously call our Ten Commandments for the postpartum mother:

1. Thou shalt not cook, clean house, do laundry, or entertain.
2. Thou shalt be given a doula (a helper, house-keeper, someone to take care of the mother).
3. Thou shalt not give up thy baby to unfamiliar caregivers.
4. Thou shalt remain clothed in thy nightgown and sit in thy rocking chair.
5. Thou shalt honor thy husband with his share of household chores.
6. Thou shalt take long walks in green pastures, eat good food, and drink much water.
7. Thou shalt not have before you strange and unhelpful visitors.

8. Thou shalt groom thy hair and adorn thy body with attractive robes.
9. Thou shalt sleep when baby sleeps.
10. Thou shalt not have before you prophets of bad baby advice.

At no time in history have new mothers been expected to do so much for so many with so little help. In most societies a new mother is given a doula, a servant who specializes in "mothering the new mother," relieving her of all the household chores that divert her energy from taking care of herself and her new baby. Centuries of tradition have taught these cultures how important it is for mother and baby to have this opportunity to get the right start. In my experience counseling parents who get off to the wrong start, it is usually not the incessant demands of a new baby that wears new parents out; it is trying to do too much too soon. Consider the terms maternity and paternity *leave*—leaving everything else to someone else and concentrate on your baby.

Most parents are not adequately prepared for how much care a newborn baby requires. The first couple of weeks are usually described as "wonderful but draining." Your body is undergoing tremendous changes, adjusting from having just given birth and preparing to continue nourishing your baby. You will experience tremendous change in your sleep schedule and eating patterns. It is extremely important to temporarily shelve and eliminate anything that may siphon off your and your baby's energy.

- **Find dad's role in the nesting period.** Dad, when mother and baby come home from the hospital or birthing place, make your "nest" as conducive to mothering as possible. Take over the housekeeping or hire some help if you can afford it. Because of the tremendous physiological and physical changes going on in the postpartum period, new mothers' emotions are very unstable. An organized environment helps foster an organized emotional state in mother and baby. It is a good idea to stroll around the house each day and take inventory of actual and potential problems that may upset the mother—and then take care of these problems! Remember that upsets felt by the mother may be transferred to the baby. An upset nest is an upset mother.

Give specific instructions to older siblings to pick up after themselves. Tell them why particular attention to tidiness is so important at this time. After all, they are future mothers and fathers; they should learn that the postpartum period is a time when the whole family gives to mom.

- **Ward off prophets of bad baby advice.** This is your baby, not someone else's. Love for her baby makes a new mother particularly vulnerable to advice that implies that she might not be doing the best thing for her baby. This is the father's opportunity to shine. If you sense that outside advice is upsetting your wife, protect her against it and support her style of mothering.

- Be open to the cues of your baby and respond according to intuitive feelings. Remember, every baby comes wired with attachment-promoting behaviors which enable him to communicate his level of need to his caregivers. Parents also come wired with a certain intuitive level of giving and responding. Part of developing the fit during the early weeks is to match the need level of the baby and the response level of the parents. Baby gives a cue, and the mother and father, because they are open and tuned into the baby, respond. In time you and your baby begin to flow together, developing a harmony between cue and response. As all members of the family repeatedly rehearse this communication, the baby learns to cue better, the parents learn to respond better, and the family learns to fit.

15

~~~~~~

CHOOSING THE RIGHT FORMULA FOR YOUR BABY

For mothers who choose to bottlefeed or who for medical reasons are unable to breastfeed, selecting the right formula is a very important decision. Although I believe that breastfeeding is the optimal design for infant nutrition, the commercially-prepared infant formulas are relatively safe and effective as an alternative source of nutrition for most infants. All infant feeding is both an art and a science, formula-feeding as well as breastfeeding.

The art of formula-feeding. Feeding your baby is not only a source of nutrition, it is a developmental and social interaction. There should always be a person at both ends of the bottle interacting with one another during the feeding. Do not put your infant in a crib and prop the bottle on a rolled-up towel so your infant can self-feed. This practice is dangerous because it might induce choking; it is also not a wise parenting habit. Relate with your baby during bottlefeeding, just as you would with breastfeeding. Look at, touch, caress, and talk with your baby during nursing (I use the term nursing in a general way to mean feeding and comforting, not only breastfeeding). Studies have shown that newborns settle best when they have small, frequent feeding, rather than rigidly scheduled large and less frequent feedings; avoid the tendency to fill the baby up in hopes that she will sleep longer and require less caregiving energy from you. Feeding time is a better bonding time if you undress yourself and your baby and hold him in close skin-to-skin contact on your breasts even though you are bottlefeeding. What's important is not only the kind of milk your infant gets but how he gets it. If you develop creative feeding techniques of holding and relating with your baby during the feeding, both of you will look forward to this special time. Although the milk is called an artificial formula, it should be a very human style of feeding.

The science of formula-feeding. Because formula is a static nutrient and breast milk is a dynamically changing nutrient, formula is second-best. Formulas are prepared using cow's milk or certain legumes, such as soy bean, as nutrient base. Vitamins, minerals, iron and chemically-produced portions of various nutrients are added to "humanize" the infant formula.

You and your doctor can choose a formula that is least likely to induce an allergic reaction in your baby. There are generally three types of formulas, categorized according to the allergenicity of the protein base used. The following types of formulas are listed in order of descending allergenicity:

1. Cow's milk-based formulas with a protein base of modified cow's milk
2. Soybean-based formulas with a protein base of soybean
3. Predigested or hypoallergenic formulas, in which the proteins are predigested to make them less allergic. Some of these predigested formulas can be very expensive and may have an unpleasant taste.

How much and how often? The amount of formula your infant drinks depends on his weight and his appetite.

However, you can use the following rule of thumb: By the end of the first week, a full-term baby usually takes around three to four ounces every three to four hours, and by age one month baby may be taking between two and two and a half ounces of formula per pound per day. For example, if your baby weighs ten pounds, he may take 20 to 25 ounces of formula per day. This amount may change from day to day. It is wise to offer the formula-fed baby at least one bottle of water each day, because formula is more concentrated than breast milk and the water helps the immature kidneys process the formula better. Additional water may also alleviate the constipating effect of most formulas.

Feeding schedule. In demand feeding an infant is fed every time he or his little tummy desires; in scheduled feeding a baby is fed every three to four hours at preassigned times according to mother's convenience and baby's appetite. A third alternative is the semi-demand schedule in which your baby has one or two preassigned feedings and is fed on demand between them. Formula-fed babies can be put on a schedule more easily since formula is digested more slowly. Demand feeding caters to your infant's satisfaction; scheduled feeding is for your convenience and your own individual family situation. Most formula-feeding mothers elect the compromise of a semi-demand type of schedule. During the first few weeks they wake their babies for feedings during the day, if the babies sleep more than four or five hours, in order to discourage the exhausting feeding pattern of a day sleeper and night feeder. Frequent feedings during the day and bottles at 7 P.M. and 11 P.M. seem to be the most comfortable feeding schedule for most parents.

Vitamins and fluoride supplements. Commercial formulas contain all the vitamins necessary for your infant, but remember that in order for your baby to receive the daily recommended amount of vitamins, he has to take the entire can of formula. Most babies do not consume an entire can of formula every day until they are a few months old, so your doctor may recommend vitamin supplements. Fluoride supplements may or may not be prescribed by your physician depending on how much fluoride is in your drinking water and whether you use fluoride-supplemented water to mix with the formula.

Formula-fed infants should receive iron-fortified formulas from birth on, or at least from four months on. Iron is necessary to make new red blood cells and to replenish the used-up iron that came from your blood in the womb. Parents may feel that the added iron causes gastrointestinal upsets in their infants, although controlled studies comparing iron-fortified formulas and formulas without iron show no difference in the number of intestinal problems. Iron-fortified formulas often give a baby's stool a green color, but this has no significance.

Choosing the right formula. Your doctor should help you choose the best formula for your baby. In recent years a few formula companies have advertised directly to the general public, going against the time-honored and respected custom of considering formula a medical substance and therefore not to be advertised directly to the public. The American Academy of Pediatrics has taken a strong stand against this type of direct advertising since parents may use less than optimal nutritional information to make their decisions.

Commercial formulas are available in three forms: powdered formula with directions for adding water, concentrated liquid formula mixed half-and-half with water, and ready-to-feed formulas that can be poured directly into a bottle. Your choice of formula is mainly a question of economics, powdered formulas being the least expensive and ready-to-feed the most costly. A word of caution: **Never mix the formula in a greater strength than the directions advise.** Always add the specified amount of water. Adding too little water makes the formula too concentrated for your newborn's kidneys and intestines to handle and may make him sick. Babies usually like their formula slightly warmed, like breast milk. Iron-fortified formulas should be used unless your doctor advises otherwise.

Signs that your infant may be allergic to the formula are colicky symptoms or fussiness immediately after the feeding; frequent vomiting, bloating or gas in the abdomen; frequent acid-burn diaper rashes (see Key 28 for description of this type of rash); frequent night waking; a red, raised, sandpaper-like rash on the face; watery diarrhea; and, sometimes failure to thrive. If you or your doctor suspect a formula allergy, switch to a less allergic formula according to the list above. Some abdominal discomfort may be caused by feeding a baby too much formula at any one feeding. Signs of overfeeding are vomiting and/or diarrhea immediately after the feeding and abdominal discomfort. Smaller, more frequent feedings with frequent burping during and after the feeding may help. You may also try to experiment with various types of nipples and infant feedings systems (bottles and nipples that minimize air swallowing). Also be sure the nipple hole is large enough. Normally the nipple hole should allow formula to drip out of a full unshaken bottle at least one drop per second.

How to burp your baby. Burping baby implies two interactions: upright position and pressure on his tummy. Hold your baby upright on your lap and let him lie forward against the heel of your hand; then press against his tummy just above the navel while you gently pat his back. You may also drape baby over your knee with his abdomen pressing on your thigh and pat his back, but this position often encourages too much spitting up. You may also try the shoulder burp by placing your baby's abdomen over your shoulder and patting his back (if you don't mind spit-up on your clothing). Usually the lap burp works best and is more convenient.

Following these principals of both the art and the science of formula-feeding your baby should help both of you thrive during these special times of infant feedings.

16

DECIDING WHETHER
TO HAVE YOUR BABY
CIRCUMCISED

Until recent years circumcision was considered a routine procedure for most newborn males in the United States, but parents are beginning to ask if it is really necessary for their babies. The American Academy of Pediatrics has taken the stand that routine circumcision is an unnecessary procedure. The following questions and answers are intended to help you make this decision.

1. **How is circumcision performed?** The baby is placed on a restraining board, and his hands and feet are secured by straps. The tight adhesions between the foreskin and the penis are separated with a metal instrument. The foreskin is held in place with metal clamps while a cut is made into the foreskin to about one-third of its length. A metal bell is placed over the head of the penis, and the foreskin is pulled up over the bell and cut circumferentially. About one-third of the skin of the penis (called the foreskin) is removed.

2. **Is circumcision safe? Does it hurt?** Circumcision is usually a very safe surgical procedure, and there are rarely any complications. However, as with any surgical procedure, there are occasional problems, such as bleeding, in-

fection, or injury to the penis. Yes, it does hurt. The skin is clamped and cut; of course it hurts! A newborn baby has painful sensations in the skin of his penis, and it is unrealistic to convince yourself that this procedure does not hurt. As a withdrawal reaction from the pain, many babies initially cry and fall into a deep sleep toward the end of the operation.

3. **Can the baby have anesthesia to lessen the pain?** Yes, a local anesthesia can be used. Ask your doctor about this. Although many physicians do not use local anesthesia, painless circumcision should be a birthright. If your doctor is not aware of this technique, he or she can find a description of the local anesthesia procedure in the *Journal of Pediatrics*, 1978, Vol. 92, page 998.

4. **Does circumcision make hygiene easier?** The glands in the foreskin secrete a fluid called smegma. These secretions may accumulate beneath the foreskin and occasionally irritate the penis, although it very rarely becomes infected. Removing the foreskin removes the secretions and makes care of the penis easier. However, with normal bathing an intact foreskin is really quite easy to care for.

5. **What happens if the foreskin is left intact?** At birth it is impossible to make a judgment about how tight the foreskin will remain, since almost all boys have tight foreskins for the first few months. By one year of age in about 50 percent of boys, the foreskin loosens from the head of the penis and retracts completely.

By three years of age, 90 percent of uncircumcised boys have fully retractable foreskins. Once the foreskin retracts easily, it becomes a normal part of male hygiene to pull back the foreskin and cleanse beneath it during a bath. Above all, do not forcibly retract the foreskin; allow it to retract naturally over a period of years. Retracting the foreskin before its time loosens the protective seal and increases the chance of infection. I call this the "uncare" of the foreskin.

6. **If the foreskin does not retract naturally, will he need a circumcision later on?** Circumcision is very rarely necessary for medical reasons, but occasionally the foreskin does not retract, becomes tight and infected, and obstructs the flow of urine. This unusual condition, called phimosis, requires circumcision. However, if circumcision for phimosis is necessary later in childhood or adulthood, an anesthetic is given and the boy is involved in the decision process.

7. **If he isn't circumcised, won't he feel different from his friends?** Parents cannot predict how their son will feel. Children generally have a wider acceptance of individual differences than adults do. It is difficult to predict whether the majority of boys will be circumcised or intact in the future. The number of circumcised boys has been steadily declining in recent years as more parents begin to question routine circumcision. I suspect that over the next decade about half the boys will be circumcised and half will be left intact.

8. **My husband is circumcised, so shouldn't my son be the same as his father?** Fathers and sons seldom compare foreskins. It used to be the custom "like father like son." However, even fathers (usually because of pressure from their wives) are beginning to question the necessity of routine circumcision.

9. **Should brothers in the same family be the same?** Many parents feel that sameness is very important among the males in the family; however, like fathers and sons, brothers seldom compare the style of their penises. Your problem most likely is not in explaining to your intact child why he is intact but rather in explaining to your circumcised child why he is circumcised.

10. **Do circumcised boys experience any particular problems?** The foreskin acts as a protective covering of the sensitive head of the penis. Removal of the protective foreskin allows the head of the penis to come in contact with ammonia in the diapers. Sometimes this irritation causes circumcised babies to develop painful sores on the tip of the penis that may obstruct the flow of urine.

11. **Does circumcision prevent any disease?** Circumcision does not prevent cancer of the penis. Cancer of the penis is a very rare disease anyway, and it occurs more frequently in males who do not practice proper hygiene. Circumcision does not prevent cervical cancer. Circumcision also does not prevent venereal disease.

In the above discussion, I have presented to you my opinion that routine circumcision is not medically indicated. Your individual family custom and desires should be respected.

If you choose to leave your baby's foreskin intact, follow these suggestions on its care. In most babies the foreskin is tightly adhered to the underlying head of the penis during the first year; do not retract the foreskin before its time. The age at which the foreskin begins to retract varies considerably from baby to baby; respect this difference and do not risk prematurely breaking the seal between the foreskin and the head of the penis, which may allow secretions to accumulate beneath the foreskin and cause infection. As the foreskin naturally retracts (usually around the third year), gently clean out the secretions that may have accumulated between the foreskin and the glans of the penis. This should be done as part of the child's normal bath routine. Usually by three years of age, when most foreskins are fully retracted, a child can be taught to clean beneath his foreskin as part of his normal bath routine.

17

~~~~~~

NAMING YOUR BABY

One of the most important decisions you will make for your child is the name you give. It's a life-long label, so choose it with care. The following are some general considerations in naming your baby.

Deciding on a name. Some parents have great difficulty deciding on a name. Since this is a major decision, take your time. Try the name on for a while to see if it fits. It is reasonable to preselect a few of your favorite names and over the first days or weeks try one or more names to see which one best fits the temperament of your baby. After you have lived with the name for a few days, you will have a feeling of whether this particular name fits your child. If not, change it as quickly as you can. We did this with our seventh baby. He was David for the first three days. It didn't feel right so we changed it to Stephen, our alternate choice, and stayed with that. Let your other children live with the name for a while to see if the whole family likes the name. One parent in my practice had great difficulty naming her fifth baby. Since she was sure that "five is *enough*," this baby was known as Nuffy for the first six months.

Meanings of names. In many cultures names have symbolic meanings. In my pediatric practice I have a list of beautiful names that have meanings. These are usually from parents of Oriental or Middle Eastern descent. Most of these names have to do with uplifting mind and body characteristics such as "Beautiful intelligent one." Be sure to convey the meaning to your child later on, as it adds a bit of depth to his or her name.

Using family names. In our family we consider it a beautiful custom to honor a beloved grandparent by giving the child either the first or middle name of the grandparent. Sometimes even last names of treasured family members are used as a middle name. Our sixth child, Matthew Robinson Sears, is named for his late greatgrandmother Robinson. It may be unwise to choose a name that neither fits the child nor is compatible with the adjacent first, second, or last name just to please the family. Think of your child first and family second. If you use a very unusual family name as either a first or second name, it is wise to couple it with a more familiar first name. This gives the child the option of choosing which name he or she is most comfortable with later on. My second name is Penton, the last name of a distant grandmother. Up until high school, my parents called me by my middle name, but I was known by my friends as Penny, a nickname I kept throughout high school. When entering college I dropped the middle name, using only the middle initial P, so that no one knew my middle name and I was henceforth called Bill for my first name, William.

Name rhythms. Using names with an equal number of syllables creates pleasing rhythms. William Penton Sears has three, two, and one syllables. A short monosyllable first and last name deserves a more drawn out middle name, e.g., Mark Anthony Smith.

Beware of joke names. Children are ruthless in what they can make out of a child's name. Beware of rhymes and unusual initials that guarantee future embarrassment. *N*olan *E*van *R*udolph *D*aner is a set-up for the child being known as N.E.R.D.

Discourage unusual or ambiguous spellings. I have always loved the name Aimee, but we decided against this name for either of our girls since she would go through life having to spell her name Amy or Aimee. In some ways, an idiosyncratic spelling may give specialness to the name if the child doesn't mind the spelling nuisance. If this is a consideration combine it with an unambiguous name for which there is only one spelling, so the child can later choose.

Combine an unusual name with a more traditional compatible name. One of our daughters is named Heather Hayden Sears (Hayden after one of our favorite greatgrandmothers). She is now 12 years old and still goes by Hayden, but she has the option of changing it to Heather. Our seventh child, Stephen, will probably always have to spell his name to distinguish it from Steven, but he will just have to learn to live with that because we like that name, it fits, and we like the spelling.

Juniors, etc. While naming a child after his father or grandfather is an old custom, be prepared for possible confusion in the family about who is meant when you call the name. Usually, families are forced to develop nicknames; if a father is Bill, the son will probably be Billy. But that Billy is going to grow up and want to be called Bill. Then what do you do—label the men in the family old Bill and young Bill, big Bill and little Bill? This may not sit well with either man; old Bill wants to look and act younger, and little Bill wants to be bigger. For grandfather, father, and son to have the same name is a beautiful family custom—as long as all are prepared to be a little bit flexible with the inconvenience at family reunions.

A name is a name is a name. Give it wise consideration, for it is the most important label your child will ever receive.

18

WHAT NEWBORNS CAN SEE

People used to believe that newborns don't see or hear much and that all they do is sleep and eat. We now know that newborns see a lot, hear a lot, and have many more capabilities than we used to give them credit for.

What your newborn can see. Within a few hours after birth your newborn's eyes become less sensitive to the brightness of the world he has just entered, but he may continue to squint during sudden changes, such as going into bright sunlight from a dimly lit room. During the first few days babies' eyes are closed most of the time, which can be very frustrating to parents. Here is a little eye-opening trick I use during newborn examinations: Hold your baby in front of you with one hand supporting his head and the other hand under his bottom, and hold his head approximately 12 inches from your eyes. Turning from the waist, swing him gently in an arc of about 120 degrees and come to a slightly abrupt stop. This rotating motion prompts baby to open his eyes reflexively. Another method is to support your baby's head and bottom and raise him gently from a lying to a sitting position.

Recent experiments have shown that the newborn can see much better than previously thought. Newborn babies can focus best at a distance from 8 to 12 inches, which corresponds to the usual eye-to-eye distance during breastfeeding. A newborn's visual acuity is estimated to be 30/20, which means that a newborn can see clearly at 20 feet what an adult with normal vision can see clearly at 30 feet.

Newborns like to look at the human face, the real thing or drawing or photos of the face. Next in order of preference are black-and-white contrasting patterns—checkerboards, stripes, (at least a half inch wide), and bull's-eyes. Bear this in mind when designing your baby's nursery. For babies, black and white is in. While pastel colors are favored by designers, babies have never been consulted. If they had been, they would have chosen more dark and light contrasting patterns.

A fun exercise with your baby is to watch her eyes tracking, that is, following an object or person with her eyes moving from side to side. Some newborns can follow an interesting object or person with their eyes from side to side for nearly 180 degrees. If the object moves too fast or is more than 12 inches away, they quickly lose interest. Because the tonic neck reflex keeps their heads turned toward one side, most newborns follow a moving object for only 90 degrees from one side to center before losing interest and turning away. Your newborn's eyes and head movements do not work well together. If you turn your baby's head, her eyes will follow slowly. If her eyes follow your face, her head rotation is somewhat jerky, as if the head is trying to catch up. Synchronous head and eye rotation does not occur until around age one month.

Fixating. You will notice that your newborn's eyes often wander independently and are crossed. While experiments have shown that newborns have the capability to coordinate both eyes momentarily, they usually don't do it all the time. Because they do not use both eyes together, images do not fall in the same part of the retina in each eye, resulting in poor depth perception. As babies learn to hold their heads and eyes still and coordinate their eye movements, images become clear and depth perception improves. This is called binocular vision and starts to develop around six weeks, becoming well-established by four months. You may notice that your newborn's eyes occasionally fixate on yours, though only for a fleeting second or two. If you hold your face within baby's focal distance (12 inches) when he is in the state of quiet alertness, he may look steadily at your eyes for five to ten seconds. During the first few weeks, when baby's eyes search and scan and are seldom still, parents often plead with the baby to "look at me." Baby does finally look at you a bit longer around two weeks of age, often around the time he begins to smile in reaction to someone's gestures. Even though babies begin to focus around two weeks, their eyes continue to move independently most of the time and to lag behind the head when it is rotated from side to side, a phenomenon called "dolls' eyes." This response disappears by two or three months. A noticeable increase in staring and enlargement of the pupil size are other changes in vision that occur around two weeks of age.

A newborn baby has a limited ability to protect his eyes. He blinks in response to a startling noise or flash of light but does not blink protectively when an object moves toward his eyes. This protective ability develops sometime during the second month.

During the first month newborns tend to be scanners and look at the edges of the face rather than at central figures. During the second or third month, you may notice that your newborn is much more interested in your eyes, nose, and mouth—the features at the center of your face. The eye itself has qualities that appeal to newborns: shininess and light-and-dark contrast. Babies are also fascinated by small moving objects like the eye. Similarly, mother's breasts are round and have contrasting light and dark areas that may naturally appeal to babies. Studies have shown that patterns stimulate sucking in the newborn. Perhaps this is why newborn babies suck better while looking at their mother's faces (older babies may be distracted by visual stimuli and actually stop sucking).

How widely a baby's eyes are open and the characteristics of his body tone give a cue to his state of relaxation and receptivity to playful interaction.

Relating to your baby visually. When you want to play your favorite eye games with your newborn, wait for her to be in that state of quiet alertness that is the best behavioral state for any form of playful interaction. Newborns pay the most attention to images that have the characteristics of the human face: contrasting light and dark areas, almost constant motion, constantly changing patterns, roundness, and responsiveness to the infant's actions. The constantly changing expression of the human face retains baby's interest longest, especially faces with mustaches and beards; the light-dark contrast between the hair and skin holds baby's attention. As early as two weeks of age, a baby watches his mother's face longer than that of a stranger.

By the end of the first month you will be amazed at the holding power you have when enjoying these facial games with your baby.

19

WWWWWWWWWWWWWWWWWWWWWWWWWWWWWWWWWWWWWWWWWWWWWWWWW

WHAT NEWBORNS
CAN HEAR

Your newborn baby probably hears as well as an adult, but there are some things new parents should note about newborn hearing. Newborn babies are more sensitive to loud and startling sounds; they may blink, jerk, or draw in their breath sharply. You will notice that your baby reacts differently to different sounds. While he may startle or shudder at loud, sharp noises, soft crooning noises produce fleeting smiles. Newborns prefer higher pitched voices and are often soothed more easily by mother's high-pitched voice than by father's lower-pitched one. Babies are also selective in their musical tastes. They calm when they hear classical music that has a regular rhythm and gentle dynamics. Music that has rapid volume changes or is just plain too loud (like rock and roll) may make them startle or just tune out. (At this writing, my wife and I have seven children with varying degrees of musical taste and, unfortunately, affinities for varying intensities of volume. I have concluded that a child's musical taste often deteriorates from infancy through adolescence.)

Newborns have a remarkable quality for protecting themselves from unpleasant noises. They can selectively block out disturbing noises. This is called a stimulus barrier. Because of it, you may find it difficult to test your baby's hearing. Sometimes babies simply do not react to a loud noise, while at other times they do. Also, newborns have difficulty concentrating on two activities at once. If baby is intently nursing, he may seem oblivious to noise. Early in the newborn period, the stimulus barrier is more pronounced, but toward the end of the first month babies seem to react more to a noisy environment.

Mothers are often confused about whether their babies hear them. The baby may not turn his head toward the sound of your voice for two or three months. Also, babies who are with their mothers constantly may become habituated to their mothers' voices; a baby hears his mother's voice so often that he stops reacting every time she speaks. However, studies have shown that the newborn baby can distinguish his own mother's voice from that of a stranger. When researchers placed babies 20 to 30 days old behind a screen so that they could hear the voices but could not see the speaker, the babies sucked faster and longer in response to their own mothers' voices than in response to those of strangers.

Newborn babies soon learn that mother's voice comes from her mouth. In one study, a mother spoke to her baby through a glass screen. The baby could see the mother through the glass but could hear her only by means of two stereo speakers, one on each side of the baby. The balance between the speakers could be adjusted so that the sound appeared to come from straight ahead or from the sides. The babies in the study were content when the sound appeared to come from straight ahead, i.e., from the mother's mouth, but they were disturbed if the sound came from another direction.

How your baby learns to talk. Even as early as one day of age your newborn may move in synchrony with your voice and speaking gestures. This early body language is the beginning of your baby's speech. During the first month, you may not consciously notice any reaction from your baby when you speak to her, but she does react even though the reaction may be imperceptible to your eyes. Researchers who analyzed films frame by frame noticed that the listening baby seemed to move in time to the rhythm of mother's voice. As the mother spoke, the infant made slight but constant movements of the head, eyes, shoulders, arms, hands, and feet. Remarkably, these movements started, stopped, or changed in almost perfect synchrony with mother's speech. Further analysis of these high-speed films showed that infants are highly sensitive to differences in sounds within the same word. For example, babies showed three distinct responses to the three basic sounds (phonemes) in *over*—the *o*, the *v*, and the *er*. Because your baby's reaction to your speech during the first month is so subtle, you do not usually realize that you are getting through to the baby. Speech should be a naturally occurring interaction, not one that you have to teach yourself to initiate. Mothers instinctively use upbeat tones and facial gestures to talk to babies. They E-X-A-G-G-E-R-A-T-E. The sing-song quality of mother's speech is tailored to the baby's listening abilities. Mothers speed up and slow down. Vowel duration is longer—"Gooood, baaaaby." Mothers talk in slowly rising crescendos and decrescendos, with bursts and pauses, allowing the baby some time to process each short vocal package before the next communication begins. How a mother talks to her baby is more important than what she says.

Analysis of mother-baby communication shows that what seems to be a monologue by the mother is really an imaginary dialogue. Although the infant rarely vocalizes back, the mother generally behaves as if he had. She naturally shortens her message and elongates her pauses; the length of the pauses coincides with the length of the imagined response of the infant, especially when she is talking to the baby in the form of questions. In this early "taking turns" type of speech, mother is shaping the infant's responses. He will store this information away and use it later when he becomes truly verbal.

In the first month, mother-baby talk is more for bonding than for exchange of information. Talk to your baby a lot, even if you feel self-conscious at first. Talk to her about what you are doing and tell her about yourself. Get used to addressing your baby by name—"Hi, Jessica!" If you use your baby's name frequently, she will soon recognize it. You will engage her attention more quickly and hold it longer if you open your dialogue with her name and repeat it frequently during the conversation. While she does not yet associate the name with herself, hearing it frequently triggers associations with the special sounds that she has heard before. She perks up and pays attention, much like adults do when they hear a familiar tune.

Getting to know your baby during the first month is an exciting, interesting, and sometimes exhausting process. Discovering her capabilities right from the start makes your parenting job easier and more enjoyable in the months—and years—to come.

20

~~~~~~

THE NEWBORN'S CRY

Although well-meaning friends and relatives frequently advise you to let your baby cry it out, nearly all the mothers I have interviewed have responded, "I just can't," or "It just doesn't feel right to me." The reason mothers can't and the reason it doesn't feel right is because it is not right.

When you let your baby cry, both members of your communication network lose. A baby's cry is a signal that she needs attention. The cry also triggers a powerful urge in the mother to pick up and comfort her baby.

To advise a mother to let her baby cry it out is not only to defy all laws of common sense but it goes against a mother's biology. On the other hand, responding promptly to a baby's cries accomplishes two things. First, it lessens a baby's need to cry by enabling him to develop a sense of trust in his environment. This trust lessens a baby's overall fretfulness. It also teaches him to "cry better." If a crying baby is left unattended, baby learns to cry harder and develops a more disturbing crying pattern—the sounds that drive parents up the wall. Babies whose cries are responded to promptly develop a crying pattern that is easier to listen to and promotes in the listener a sensitive desire to comfort the baby.

Responding promptly to your baby's crying and the bodily changes that precede it also increases your sensitivity to her cues, so that gradually you learn to anticipate her crying, instead of only responding to it. Thus, you also work to reduce her crying.

One of the popular myths about responding to the crying baby is that the baby will learn to manipulate you and become a crybaby. Wrong! Studies have shown that babies who are given a prompt and nuturant response to their cries early on later become less clingy babies and cry less. Don't worry about being manipulated later on. Respond to your newborn's cries as promptly and as sensitively as you can. Later on your baby will develop noncrying ways of communicating, and your response time will intuitively lengthen. Because your newborn learns to trust, she will become better able to accept your delayed response. However, the infant who has received an inconsistent response to her cries early on does not learn to trust and later becomes anxious about her environment. She does not learn to trust her cues nor does she learn to trust the response. An untrusting infant is likely to cry more. Respond promptly to your baby's cries. It is good language for both of you.

Spoiling is discussed in detail in Key 22.

Cry-stoppers that work. The following are time-tested comforting methods that lessen your baby's need to cry and lower the frequency and intensity of your baby's cries.

1. Room in with your baby. This usually results in babies who cry less and mothers who learn a comfortable and sensitive nurturant response to their baby's cries.
2. Wear your baby. Carry your newborn in a sling-type carrier as much as possible, preferably around three hours per day. Studies have shown that babies who are carried at least three hours a day cry nearly 50 percent less.

3. Feed your baby on cue rather than on schedule.

4. Try **motion** to soothe your newborn. Remember, your baby has been used to moving for nine months. If the usual cry-stoppers don't work and you are at your wits' end, put your baby in a car seat and take a long nonstop car ride. Nearly once a week I receive a call from frantic new parents unable to stop the cries of their newborn. This "freeway therapy" nearly always works.

Your baby's cry is one of the most meaningful sounds you will ever hear. Listen to it, respond to it; it will soon pass. For more detailed information on how to mellow your baby's cry, see Barron's *Keys to Calming the Fussy Baby* in this series.

21

~~~~~~

UNDERSTANDING YOUR NEWBORN'S TEMPERAMENT

Mothers often get a clue to their baby's temperament in the womb. Very active babies, "kickers," often stimulate thoughts of "I've got a real live wire on my hands." Even in the newborn nursery, babies receive early labels regarding temperament. As director of a newborn nursery I advised the nurses not to judge quickly the person this newborn would later become. It is true, however, that newborn babies often give us a clue as to their later temperaments. The reason that it is important for parents to understand their newborn's temperament is it helps them to match their parenting style to that temperament.

Picture the newborn baby who cries every time he is put in his bassinet. The parents are constantly picking the baby up; as soon as they do he stops crying. This baby is often unfairly labeled fussy. A better term than fussy is "high-need baby." Some babies give parents a clue as to what they need even in the first few days of life. To understand why high-need babies have the temperament they do, which is crucial in helping you get the right start with this special type of baby, you must understand *the need level concept.* Every baby comes with a certain level of need which, if met, allows the infant to develop to her maximum potential. Every baby also comes with a corresponding temperament to alert the caregiver to that level of needs. For example, the newborn who cries every time she is put down in her crib or bassinet, who feeds continuously during the day, and who settles with difficulty at night often is labelled as fussy, difficult, or colicky. If you are blessed with this of baby, you have a "high-need baby." This is a kinder term and more accurately portrays the temperament of the baby and the level of parenting she needs. Then there is the easy baby (those you read about or that your friends have) who sleeps through the night, lies contentedly in his crib much of the day, schedules easily, and fusses little. Consider how the need levels of these two temperaments play a part in determining different styles of parenting. The high-need baby fusses every time you put him down because inherent in this baby is a high level of need to be held and the temperament that causes him to fuss if he is put down. If this baby is held a lot, he will develop to his maximum potential. If the high-need baby needs to be held a lot but does not have the temperament to alert caregivers that he needs this, it is possible that he will receive a lower level of care than he requires and will not develop to his maximum potential. The easy baby, on the other hand, may sleep longer, cry less, and not fuss when put down. This baby is likely to be held less because he demands less attention.

Each of these babies is likely to elicit different parenting styles from their caregivers. The high-need baby is held more often because she demands it, is fed more often because she demands it, and is picked up more often because she demands it. The high-need baby brings out in her caregivers a higher level of parenting. She receives and deserves the label "demanding" very early in life because her temperament requires her to be demanding to achieve the level of parenting that she needs. In some ways the high-need baby is easier than the easy baby because parents know where they stand. The easy baby, because he is less demanding, may not get held as much, fed as often, and interacted with as often. It is the high-need babies who often gets the higher standard of care—because they demand it.

Then there is the easy baby in high-need baby disguise—the easy baby who actually needs to be held and fed more often and carried most·of the time but does not have the temperament to demand this higher level of care. Parents, beware of the "too-good baby" who may be a high-need baby in easy-baby disguise. I have frequently seen this "good baby" become very fussy after the first two or three weeks of being relatively content. If easy babies are held a lot, fed on cue, and picked up when they cry, they often remain easy and do not become fussy babies, simply because they don't have to.

Flexibility is the key toward parenting your baby according to his or her own temperament. If you go with the flow of your baby's temperament and match your level of giving to the need level of your baby, you will better develop better caregiving skills and your baby will better develop her temperament. Matching the temperament of the baby and the giving level of the parents helps both of you enjoy each other more.

22

~~~~~~

FEAR OF SPOILING

Some parents worry that by holding baby most of the time, feeding him on cue, and picking him up every time he cries, they will spoil him. Nonsense! Perhaps an explanation of the background that has caused parents to fear spoiling their baby will help you understand how this unfounded theory became so popular. Between 1920 and 1960 an unfortunate parenting style that I call detachment parenting became popular. So-called experts developed theories that gradually detached mothers from babies. First, birth became more a surgical operation than a normal physiologic process. Mothers were separated from their babies after birth, and babies were cared for by "experts" in the nursery. The next step in mother-infant detachment was the promotion by formula manufacturers of "humanized" artificial formulas as a substitute for breast milk, convincing mothers that it was just as good and certainly more convenient. The next disruption of the mother-infant continuum came when advisers warned mothers not to sleep with their babies. Finally, in the 50s and 60s, a behavioristic school of thought that preached that parents should restrain themselves from responding to the baby's cries became popular. Unfortunate and unfounded theories of baby care were coupled with economic necessity that resulted in more and more mothers leaving their babies in day care. The end result of these detachment styles was that parents did not know their babies. They were separated at birth, separated from the breast, separated by night and separated by day. Mothers were advised to go against biological instincts that urged them to give a nurturant response to baby's cry.

In essence, parents lost confidence in themselves and turned child rearing over to experts.

The reality, however, is that experts did not know. Somewhere during this age of detachment, the spoiling theory—the idea that if you responded intuitively and were closely attached to your baby, the baby would be spoiled, that is, terminally dependent on the parents—became popular. Finally, in the early 70s mother's intuition began bucking these spoiling theories. In addition, well-respected child psychologists began comparing infants reared in this detachment style with infants reared by attachment parenting. Not surprisingly, they found that infants who grew up with a close attachment to their parents (bonded at birth, breastfed on cue, given a nurturant response to cries, carried a lot, and often allowed to sleep with their parents) actually turned out to be more independent and less clingy and separated more easily from their parents sometime during the second year. Scientific studies have finally proven what mothers have suspected all along—that close parental attachment to babies does not spoil. As one mother of a very attached and independent child exclaimed, "She's not spoiled, she's fresh!"

There are two reasons why attachment parenting does not lead to spoiling. First, because parents are closely attached to their baby, they know their baby and are able to read the baby's cues; they intuitively know when to respond and when to hold off a bit. Second, because a baby has grown up in a secure environment, baby learns to trust. Trust leads to an inner feeling of rightness that allows the baby the inner security to separate more easily from the parents. In fact, one could make a case that babies who have grown up with the detachment style of parenting may actually be the spoiled babies—babies may spoil by being left alone, not by being attached.

Because of the fear of spoiling or the fear of being manipulated or because of the advice of a well-meaning friend, some mothers restrain themselves from giving a nuturant response to a baby's cries or carrying baby a lot. Even though mother's intuition tells her that she is doing right, sometimes the overwhelming desire to do what's best for baby and the fear that you may not be doing the best prompts a mother to override her intuition and give way to outside advice. The strong desire to be a good mother makes you vulnerable to any hints that you may be harming your child. Be confident in your parenting style. If the style you have chosen for your baby is working and feels right to you, you can safely turn a deaf ear to the spoiling advice.

Mothers who give way to the spoiling advice desensitize themselves to the wisdom of their intuition. Insensitivity is what gets a new mother in trouble by interfering with the mother-baby relationship. Attachment parenting, if practiced wisely during the early months, results in a certain wisdom about when to respond to your baby and when to hold off a bit. You will eventually develop a balance between giving the proper nurturing response and overindulging your baby, and this balance will come naturally.

23

~~~~~~

SELECTING A
BABY CARRIER

New research is proving what experienced mothers have known all along—that something good happens to parents and babies when they're attached. Infant development specialists have repeatedly observed that babies who are carried in a variety of cloth slings seem more content than infants who are kept in cribs, playpens, strollers, and prams. People in most cultures "wear" their babies. We call this style of parenting "baby-wearing" because it implies more than just carrying your baby; it means choosing a carrier into which you and your baby fit comfortably. In my pediatric practice, I have noticed that baby-wearing is one of the most important parenting styles you can practice. The more you wear your baby, the more content the baby will be, the more you will enjoy being with your baby, and the more you and your baby get to know each other.

Mothers in other cultures are able to wear their babies almost constantly because they fabricate a sling-type carrier that often looks like part of their garment and in fact usually is. At a recent international parenting conference I interviewed two mothers from Zambia who were wearing their babies in slings that matched their native dress. I asked them why women in their culture wear their babies so much. I received two very brief yet insightful reasons: "It makes life easier for the mother" and "It's good for the baby." After studying the whole parade of baby-wearing mothers in my practice over the last five years, I have concluded that a sling-type carrier works the best.

Selecting a baby carrier. In selecting a sling-type carrier, consider the following criteria:

- **Safety.** Safety is the most important feature of any baby carrier. The sling must both support and contain the baby. The body of the sling must be deep enough to provide a hammock contour to adequately support the head of the baby and safely contain baby's whole body. Choose a carrier by a reputable manufacturer that has been thoroughly tested and that contains the appropriate label certifying that the material complies with federal safety standards.

- **Comfort.** The carrier must be comfortable for both parents and baby. A well-designed carrier should distribute the baby's weight on the shoulders and hips of the adult, not on the back and neck. It should be well-padded over the shoulders, along the back, and wherever the edges of the carrier press against baby's torso and legs.

- **Versatility.** My personal research has shown that one of the reasons that mothers do not wear their new babies for very long is that most babies have very limited holding positions. Because of the wide range of infant weight, size, temperament, and squirminess, a well-designed sling carrier should be able to be used in a variety of ways to accommodate baby's changing size and development. A carrier should be able to be used from birth to at least two years of age, making it unnecessary to purchase a series of carriers as your baby grows. High-need babies (fussy babies, colicky babies) are seldom content to be carried in the same position all the time. Carriers that flatten babies against mother's chest are often too restrictive for a baby who, like all of us, is more content being stimulated by a 180-degree view of the world around him.

- **Ease of use.** It is a fact of human nature that if something is not convenient to use we do not use it. I find that fathers, particularly, shy away from carriers having numerous buckles and straps. As an experienced baby-wearer, I feel that it is important for baby to get used to father's handling as well as mother's. It is absolutely necessary that a carrier be easy for you to adjust while you are wearing the baby. A sling-type carrier is usually the most versatile. In the early months, the sling can be cradled against mother's chest (making nursing easier), and later on it can be carried on the hip, with baby's weight evenly distributed between the parent's shoulder and hip. Some babies like to face forward while being carried. A sling-type carrier is versatile enough to accommodate these carrying positions.

- **Suitability for breastfeeding.** With a sling-type carrier, babies can easily and discreetly breastfeed while being carried in the sling. Private breastfeeding while baby is being carried in the sling creates better harmony. A hungry baby can be quickly attached before he has to fuss vehemently; then he can then drift off quietly to a satisfied sleep.

- **Stylishness.** If a baby carrier is going to be used to the extent that I encourage mothers to wear their babies, it must be a product that the wearer finds attractive. Choose a carrier which looks good on you. Dads often shy away from patterns that appear too feminine or too cute. Many families solve this dilemma by having two slings, or they choose a compromise pattern.

A baby carrier that meets all of the above criteria is the Original Baby Sling, manufactured by Nojo. Nearly all major department stores and specialty shops carry this sling.

Safe babywearing. Observe the following safety tips when wearing your baby:

1. As you are getting used to wearing your baby, support your baby with your hands. As you be-

come accustomed to babywearing, this style will become more instinctive—like embracing your protuberant abdomen while pregnant. When baby is carried in the cradle hold, rest one arm (usually the one opposite the side of the shoulder pad) along the top rail of the sling. This added protection contains baby in case he tries to roll out of the sling. When carrying baby in the forward facing position, embrace him with your hands folded across the front of the sling, or use one hand if he is positioned off to one side. In the hip carry, be sure the top rail of the sling is pulled up over baby's back at least as high as his shoulder blades. Some babies, called archers, like to practice back dives when carried in this position. Containing baby in the sling discourages this antic.

2. Don't forget baby is in the sling. Avoid sudden twisting. Babies have fallen when mother suddenly turned to do something (e.g., rescue another baby from danger) and forgot she was wearing her baby. As a precaution, try this safety rehearsal: Suddenly twist your upper body to grab something with one hand while at the same time embracing your baby with your free hand. Rehearse this action frequently; you will instinctively clasp your baby with one hand while lunging with the other.

3. When stooping over, bend at the knees, not at the waist.

4. Do not wear baby while cooking or cycling or in a moving vehicle. The sling is not a substitute for an approved car seat.

5. Avoid backwearing in the sling. Mothers in other cultures are used to wearing their babies on their back, as if they seem to have another pair of eyes in the back of their heads. In our culture we are not used to this position, and baby may slip out of the sling without the wearer feeling the baby's danger.

6. Toddlers like to squirm and sometimes even stand in the sling. Carefully support your baby during these antics. Toddlers are now at your reaching level and can grab dangerous breakable objects off shelves. Keep an arm's distance away from potential hazards.

7. When going through doorways or around corners, be careful that baby's body does not stick out past your arm where it can strike the wall or door jamb. As a precaution, get used to keeping your body between the door or wall and baby during transit.

8. Avoid drinking or holding hot beverages while wearing your baby. Wearing your baby while eating is all right, especially if baby is sleeping. Our new baby has had a few drops of salad dressing spilled on his head; placing a napkin over baby avoids this mess.

9. Wearing your baby is a wise precaution against kidnapping while in strange crowds. Baby-wearing prevents baby-snatching.

10. Beware of carriers with small mouthable hooks, buttons, or attachments that entice baby to pull them off, mouth them, and possibly choke.

Baby-wearing is especially helpful for mothers with busy lifestyles and for postpartum mothers who are feeling a bit housebound. "Home" to a tiny baby is where you are.

24

〰〰〰〰〰〰〰〰〰〰〰〰〰〰〰〰〰〰〰〰〰〰〰〰〰〰〰〰〰〰〰

SELECTING A
SAFE CRIB

B uying a crib is one of the most emotional, and most important, steps prospective parents take as they prepare for their new baby. It can be a joyous event as you visualize your baby lying in a decorative, picture-perfect setting. However, it's important that you also keep in mind several safety factors and practical considerations.

Crib safety. My first piece of advice concerning cribs is to borrow one instead of buying. Because many babies do not sleep well in them, cribs sometimes wind up being primarily toy collectors.

Crib accidents are one of the most common and serious causes of injuries in infants, and it's vital that any crib used be a safe one. The following guidelines will help you select a safe crib. First, the crib should be painted with lead free paint. Those manufactured prior to 1974, when lead paint was made illegal for cribs, may have been painted several times with lead-containing paint; newer cribs by law must be painted with lead-free paint. If your child is a chewer, cover the guard rails with non-toxic "chew-guards." Next, check the drop sides. To prevent babies from accidentally releasing the drop sides, each one should be secured with two locking devices. The infant should not be able to release the drop sides from inside the crib. Also check the space between the bars of the crib rail. The maximum distance between the bars should be 2⅜" (6 cm), so that babies cannot get their heads caught between the bars. The bars of cribs made prior to 1979 may have wider spacing that does not conform to these standards.

As a rule, the simpler the design of the crib, the safer. Avoid cribs with decorative cut-outs and knobs. A baby's clothes can get caught on these projections, causing strangulation. Knobs and posts can be sawed off and the tops sanded smooth. Avoid cribs with ornate tops; infants have strangled in the concave space between the post and the crib. Check the crib hardware for sharp points or edges or holes or cracks where your baby's fingers could get pinched or stuck. If the baby's room is not within hearing distance of every room in the house, an intercom may prove to be a valuable safety feature.

Place the crib in a safe area of the room. The crib should not be placed against a window, near any dangling cords from blinds or draperies, or near any furniture that could be used to help the infant climb out. When your baby gets older, give some thought to what could happen if your baby does climb out of the crib: The crib should be placed so that she will not fall against any sharp object or become entrapped and possibly strangle between the crib and an adjacent wall or piece of furniture.

Bumpers and crib toys. Bumpers should run around the entire crib, tie or snap into place, and have at least six straps. To prevent your baby from chewing on the straps or becoming entangled in them, trim off any excess length. Remove bumpers and toys from the crib as soon as the child begins to pull herself up on the crib rails, because they can be used as steps for climbing over the rail. Crib toys, mobiles, pacifiers, and clothing worn in the crib should not have strings longer than eight inches.

Mattress safety. Beware of hand-me-down or second-hand mattresses that may not fit your crib exactly. To check the fit of a crib mattress, push it into one corner. There should be no more than 1½ inch (3.8 cm) gap between it and the side or end of the crib. If you fit more than two fingers between the mattress and the crib, the mattress is too small. Check the support system regularly by rattling the metal hangers and by pushing the mattress from the top and then from the bottom. If a hanger support dislodges, it needs to be fixed or replaced. Make sure the four metal hangers supporting the mattress and support board are secured into their notches by safety clips.

A final safety point about mattresses: Never leave a baby unattended in a very soft wavy waterbed. Infants have suffocated in them. The firmer, waveless type is much safer.

Pamphlets concerning crib safety are available from the U.S. Consumer Products Safety Commission's hotline (1-800-638-8326); in Maryland only, call 1-800-492-8363.

~~~~~~

25

OUTFITTING THE LAYETTE AND NURSERY

S etting up baby's nursery is a time-consuming and expensive business. There are numerous items to be purchased in advance of baby's arrival, and the temptation is to splurge to the extent your pocketbook will allow. However, it's a good idea to be sure that you have at least an adequate supply of the basics and to use restraint in how you outfit the nursery.

Nursery basics. The following lists suggest items for your newborn's early wardrobe and supplies to make caring for your baby easier:

1. Baby clothes
    - Four waterproof pants
    - Two receiving blankets
    - Lightweight tops (kimonos, sacques, and gowns)
    - Four terrycloth sleepers and/or heavyweight sacques
    - Three pairs of booties
    - Six undershirts
    - Sunhat
    - Two pairs of sox

2. Diapering needs
   - Three dozen cloth diapers (suggest diaper service)
   - Diaper liners or covers
   - Diaper pail (usually supplied by diaper service)
   - Cotton balls, cotton swabs
   - Premoistened towelettes
   - Diaper cream (zinc oxide)
   - Diaper pins
   - Black-and-white mobile to hang above changing area

3. Bathing, bedding, and medical supplies
   - Mild laundry soap
   - Mild bath soap and shampoo
   - Rectal thermometer
   - Baby bathtub, sponge, or molded bath aid
   - Rubbing alcohol
   - Petroleum jelly
   - Nasal aspirator with two-inch bulb
   - Towels and wash cloths
   - Antibacterial ointment
   - Brush and comb
   - Baby scissors
   - Flannel linens
   - Rubber-backed waterproof pads
   - Crib or bassinet sheets
   - Hooded baby blankets

4. Equipment and furnishings
   - Bassinet, cradle, crib, and accessories
   - Sling-type baby carrier
   - Changing table or padded work area
   - Diaper bag
   - Vaporizer (humidifier)
   - Rocking chair

- Reclining infant seat
- Storage chest for clothing

Cradles. Cradles are a wonderful invention. For nine months your baby has been accustomed to constant motion, so he won't like lying in a bed permanently fixed to the floor. On the other hand, as your baby shifts his weight while in a cradle, he is swayed slightly, lulling him back to a deeper sleep. Still, unless you have a family cradle that has been passed down from generation to generation and from child to child (which is a wonderful family custom), I believe in borrowing cradles. You usually use them for only four to six months, depending on how fast your baby grows and develops. The day you find your baby sitting up to peer over the cradle edge (usually by six months), you know the cradle is too small and he is ready to graduate to a crib. You may find that the switch from cradle to crib brings about some sleeping disturbances because of the absence of the rocking motion.

Decorating baby's nursery. Before you spend a lot of money and energy putting together a properly appointed nursery, remember that some high-need babies will not sleep alone in a nursery, so that the nursery becomes a catch-all for everything but baby. In my experience, the most valuable piece of baby furniture is a king-sized bed. I advise fathers to figure out what they are going to spend on a nursery, buy a king-sized bed and spend the rest on mother.

Baby furniture manufacturers have many ingenious and space-saving ideas for baby furniture. Visit a large baby-furniture store and look at the nurseries on display. Choose the one that best fits your fancy and your budget. Nearly every issue of the major baby magazines, such as *Baby Talk*, has excellent tips on outfitting your baby's nursery. These magazines are available free at most diaper services, baby stores, and doctors' offices. You will find a lot of valuable ideas in them.

100

26

wwwwwwwwwwwwwwwwwwwwwwwwwwwwwwwwwwwwwwwwwwwww

YOUR BABY'S MEDICAL CHECKUPS

T he system of well-baby care that prevails in the United States consists of periodic examinations that begin shortly after birth, continue within a week or two, and then take place every month or two thereafter until 6 months. During these well-baby exams, your health-care provider concentrates on three areas: answering any questions you have as new parents, examining your baby to be sure that he or she is growing and developing properly, and discussing growth and development during the present and subsequent stage.

Let's go through a typical newborn exam so that you can appreciate what your doctor is looking for. Your doctor forms an opinion about your baby's general health simply by looking at her. Is she alert, active, and breathing normally with good color? Does she show signs of being premature, full-term, or post-mature? Next, the doctor examines your newborn's head for any excessive molding, skull fractures, or bleeding within the scalp. Are the soft spots, the fontanels, soft and flat? Your baby's head circumference is then measured and compared to her length, weight, and maturity. Is the head proportionately large or small or of normal size? Do the baby's eyes show the normal momentary contact with the examiner's eyes? There may be a few ruptured blood vessels in the whites of the eyes; these will clear up within a few weeks. Your doctor examines the inside of your baby's eyes. The nose is then examined to see if it is formed correctly and air can pass through both nostrils. Your doctor checks inside your baby's mouth to see if the palate is fully formed. The ears are checked to be sure they are properly formed, the ear canals are open, and the ear drums appear normal. Often there are a few areas of purplish discoloration on the ear lobes, cheeks, scalp, and face after delivery.

Your doctor then checks around your baby's neck to be sure the thyroid gland is where it should be and that there are no abnormal growths. The collarbone is checked to be sure it was not broken during the squeeze of delivery. Your doctor listens to your baby's heart, records how fast it is beating, and checks for any extra heart sounds (called murmurs). Murmurs may be normal or abnormal; most are normal, caused by blood flowing through the heart very rapidly. Your doctor then checks your baby's lungs to be sure that air is going in and out properly.

Next your baby's abdomen is checked. Your doctor gently massages the baby's abdominal muscles to relax them so the liver, spleen, and kidneys can be felt to be sure that they are of normal size and normal position. Your doctor checks to make sure there are no unusual growths within the abdomen. Your baby's umbilicus is checked to make sure it is healing normally. The genitalia are checked for normal development. In the male, there is usually a large amount of water in the scrotal sack, giving the newborn's testicles a swollen appearance. In a girl, there is normally some whitish or blood-tinged vaginal discharge representing a sort of menstrual period caused by the crossover of some of the mother's hormones around the time of birth. Your baby's anus is then checked to be sure it is open and in the proper position. Your doctor checks your baby's hips to be sure the leg bones are in the hip sockets and that your baby does not have dislocated hips. While examining the hips, the doctor may feel the femoral arteries, the large vessels running through the center of the groin to the legs. The strength of the pulsation of these large arteries gives a clue about any obstruction to blood flow in the major artery coming out of the heart. Your baby's legs and feet are checked to be sure they are properly aligned. A slight amount of inward bowing of the lower legs and feet is normal, a leftover from the squatting position in utero. Your doctor then checks your baby's neurological development: reflexes, head control, muscle tone, and general level of alertness.

In addition to doing a physical check-up on your baby, your doctor reviews the birth events to see if any problems occurred that require special attention later. Your baby's blood type is usually checked and compared with mother's to see if any potential blood grouping incompatibility exists.

Periodic check-ups give your doctor a reference point for knowing your baby well, so that if your baby is sick it is much easier to make a diagnosis. Throughout the newborn period, your doctor or health-care provider gets to know your baby very well by investing time, energy, and knowledge in your baby. Therefore, if possible, use one doctor for your baby and schedule well-baby check-ups regularly.

27

~~~~~~

COMMON NEWBORN MEDICAL CONCERNS

Newborns frequently experience minor medical problems. This key describes the most common.

Eye discharge. During the first few weeks most newborns have a yellow, sticky discharge from one or both eyes. This is usually caused by a blocked tear duct. By three weeks of age most infants begin tearing, and the tears normally drain into the nose through tiny tear ducts at the inside corners of the eye. Sometimes the nasal ends of these ducts are covered by a thin membrane that should break open shortly after birth, allowing proper drainage of tears. Often, however, this membrane does not fully open, the tear ducts remain plugged, and the tears accumulate in one or both eyes. The stagnant tears become infected, resulting in yellow discharge in the corner of the eye. Treatment consists of gently massaging the tear duct that is located beneath the tiny bump in the nasal corner of each eye. Your doctor will show you how to do this. Massage in an upward direction toward the eye about six times before each diaper change. Massaging the tear duct applies pressure to the fluid trapped within the ducts and eventually pops open the membrane and clears the ducts. Your doctor may also wish to prescribe an antibiotic ointment to treat the infection. Blocked tear ducts usually clear within a few weeks to months with massage and ointment, but occasionally a blockage persists requiring an eye doctor to open these ducts by inserting a tiny wire into them. This is seldom necessary under six months of age.

Thrush. Thrush is a yeast infection in a baby's mouth that resembles cottage cheese patches on the inner lips, tongue, and roof. Because yeast thrives on milk, baby's mouth provides an ideal environment. Sometimes thrush is confused with milk deposits on the tongue and mouth. The difference is that thrush, unlike milk, cannot be easily wiped off. Thrush can be transferred to the nipples of the breastfeeding mother, causing soreness. Thrush is a very common and nonserious infection that is easily treated by painting the whitish areas with a prescription medicine.

Sniffles. In the first few months, babies' nasal passages are easily clogged with lint from blankets and clothing, dust, milk residue, or local allergens. Because the nasal passages are small in a newborn, even a slight amount of clogging can cause noisy, uncomfortable breathing. Although these sniffles sound very loud, they are not, strictly speaking, caused by a cold, that is, an infection. To clear your baby's nose, prepare some saltwater nose drops—about ¼ teaspoon of salt to 8 ounces water—or you can buy saline nose drops at the drug store. Using a plastic dropper, gently squirt a few drops in each nostril. This loosens the nasal secretions and stimulates baby to sneeze the secretions from the back of the nose toward the front, where you can gently remove them with a rubber bulb syringe. A vaporizer or humidifier in your baby's room, especially during the winter months with central heating, will help loosen the sniffles. Remove common dust collectors such as stuffed animals, feather pillows, and fuzzy blankets from your baby's sleeping environment. Above all, keep your baby away from cigarette smoke, which is one of the most common irritants to a newborn's breathing passages.

Toward the end of the first month, babies often begin making more saliva than they are able to swallow comfortably. The excess saliva pools in the back of the throat, causing

105

noisy breathing and palpable chest rattles that sound just like a cold but aren't. Baby will eventually learn to swallow this excess saliva. The noises usually lessen when babies fall asleep, because saliva slows down during sleep. Placing your baby on his stomach to sleep will allow the saliva to drool out or pool in the cheeks instead of the throat. If your baby's nasal discharge becomes increasingly thick and yellow throughout the day (nasal discharge is commonly thick in the morning because the secretions have sat stagnant in the nose all night) and is accompanied by a low grade fever, crankiness, poor feeding, and change in behavior, this is probably an infection and needs medical attention.

28

COMMON SKIN PROBLEMS IN THE NEWBORN

B abies' sensitive skin is subject to a number of minor skin problems. Most are readily treatable; none are serious.

Milia. Newborns may have tiny, whitish, pinhead-sized bumps on the nose and face. These are called milia and are caused by secretions plugging the skin pores. They are normal and with gentle washing disappear within a few weeks.

Prickly heat. This rash looks like tiny pimples with red bases and clear centers. It appears on areas of the skin where there is excessive moisture retention, often behind the ears, between the neck folds, in the groin, or in areas where clothing fits tightly. To treat it, gently wash the area in plain cool water or with a solution of baking soda (1 teaspoon to a cup of water). Also, dress your baby in lightweight, loose-fitting clothing and use a cool mist vaporizer.

Baby acne. This pimply, oily facial rash resembles teenage acne. It usually appears around the second or third week and disappears around six weeks of age if you do nothing, but gentle washing with water and a mild soap and cool mist humidity in the environment help.

Cradle cap. Cradle cap is a crusty, oily, plaque-like rash on the baby's scalp, most commonly over the soft spot. A milder form of cradle cap is more flaky, resembling dandruff. Too frequent or too vigorous hair washing only dries out the scalp and makes cradle cap worse. The dry, flaky type of cradle cap disappears if you wash the scalp less and humidify the environment. To treat the more severe, crusty type of cradle cap, massage vegetable oil into the crusty scales to soften them and then use a fine tooth comb to remove the scales. Wash off the excess oil with a mild tar shampoo, being careful to keep this away from baby's eyes. A similar crusty, oily rash may appear behind baby's ears and in the skin folds of the neck. You should wash this with warm water; a prescription cortisone cream may also help. Newborn skin enjoys high humidity, explaining why most of these rashes are worse during winter months with dry central heating. A vaporizer-humidifier in the baby's sleeping room often lessens these rashes.

Diaper rash. Diapers were invented to protect the environment from baby's excrement, and baby's skin rebels at losing its freedom to enjoy the air and sunshine. A combination of wet diaper and warm skin provides an ideal environment for the growth of bacteria that act on chemicals in the urine to produce ammonia and other skin irritants. The skin becomes inflamed, and the result is a diaper rash.

To prevent and treat your baby's diaper rash:

1. Change wet diape. s as quickly as possible.
2. During each diaper change, wash the area with plain water and mild soap, rinse well, and gently blot dry. Avoid strong soaps and excessive rubbing on sensitive skin.
3. Allow the diaper area to "breathe." Avoid tight-fitting diapers and occlusive waterproof pants that retain moisture. Reserve the waterproof

pants for times and places where a leaky diaper may be socially unacceptable. You can use rubber pads underneath your baby to protect the bedding.

4. "Air condition" your baby's diaper area. Expose your baby's bottom to the air as much as possible. While he is sleeping, unfold the diaper and lay it beneath him. In warm weather, let your baby nap outside with his bare bottom exposed to the fresh air—but avoid a sunburn.

5. Diaper creams and ointments are not necessary unless your baby's skin is irritated. Apply a barrier cream, such as zinc oxide, at the first sign of a reddened, irritated bottom. This helps protect the skin from moisture and irritants. Balmex is a good, all-around diaper cream. Treat the dia per rash early, before the skin breaks down and becomes infected. Barrier creams should also be used when your baby has diarrhea to prevent diaper rash from starting. Do not put corn starch on the area; it encourages the growth of fungi and cakes in creases.

6. Whether to use cloth or disposable diapers is a matter of convenience, sensitivity to the ecology, and baby's susceptibility to rashes. If you wash your own cloth diapers, be sure that you use the hot-wash cycle and rinse them thoroughly, then soak the washed and rinsed diapers in a solution of one cup of vinegar to half a washing-machine tub of water for a half hour. Spin the water away, and dry the diapers without further rinsing. Most busy parents find a diaper service much more convenient than washing their baby's diapers by themselves.

7. Baking soda baths are particularly helpful in treating the red, scalded, non-raised types of diaper rash called "acid burns." These are particularly common after intestinal infections or antibiotic treatment that produce acidic stools. Soak your baby's bottom in a baking soda solution, one tablespoon of baking soda to two quarts of water in the tub. After the soak, give a sniff to check for any smell of ammonia.

Sometimes it's necessary to call your doctor for a prescription. Yeast or fungus infections produce diaper rashes that are red, raised, rough, and sore looking, with tiny pustules. These are resistant to the above simple forms of treatment. Sometimes a bacterial infection is also present in these types of rashes. You may need a prescription cream containing an antifungal or antibacterial agent or cortisone; some antifungal ointments are now available over the counter. Unless otherwise instructed by your doctor, avoid using cortisone creams on the diaper area for more than seven straight days. The frequency of a baby's diaper rash is not a measure of the attentiveness of a mother. Some babies have more sensitive skin than others; no matter how frequently you change your baby's diaper, such a baby may have frequent rashes until the diapering stage is over.

Normal baby marks. Most magazine pictures of "newborns" show not newborns but babies a few months older, whose normal skin blemishes have cleared. Most newborns have smooth reddish-pink dotlike marks that are most prominent on the upper eyelids, the forehead between the eyes, and the nape of the neck. These "stork bites" are areas where blood vessels are prominent and show through the newborn's thin skin. They are called nevi (nevus means birthmark) and nearly always fade or disappear with time. Sometimes nevi on the nape of the neck persist though they are eventually covered by hair.

Some birth marks do not appear until after two or three weeks of age. The most common is called a strawberry nevus because it looks like a tiny section of a strawberry. These nevi gradually increase in size and may take as long as several years to disappear completely. Blue, bruise-like marks on the lower back or buttocks, called Mongolian spots, are very common in black, Asian, and Indian babies. These usually fade with time, but many never disappear completely. It is important for health-care providers and others to recognize that Mongolian spots are common and normal and not signs of spanking or child abuse.

29

∿∿

CARING FOR YOUR NEWBORN'S BODILY NEEDS

B abies require a good deal of care. Fortunately, providing that care is generally a lot of fun and gives you a chance for some wonderful interaction with your baby.

Cord care. Your baby's umbilical cord is usually cut to about a half-inch long and clamped. The clamp is usually removed after 24 hours. In the first few days your baby's cord may be swollen and jelly-like. It then begins to dry and shrivel up and usually falls off within a week or two. To enhance the drying of the cord and prevent infection, clean at the base of the cord with a cotton-tipped applicator dipped in alcohol or whatever antiseptic solution your doctor recommends three or four times a day. It is wise to continue cord hygiene even for a few days after the cord is completely detached. It is normal to see a few drops of blood the day the cord falls off. If your baby's cord has an increasingly offensive odor and a pus-like discharge, it may be necessary for your doctor to apply a silver nitrate solution to help dry it out. To prevent cord irritation and infection, keep the cord as dry as possible and avoid immersion baths until the cord falls off and the navel is completely dry. Do not cover the cord area with the diaper or rubber pants. If the cord becomes soiled with stools, wash it off with an alcohol-soaked cotton ball and dry it well. If the skin around your baby's cord becomes red and swollen to about the size of a silver dollar, your baby's cord may be infected and you should call your doctor.

Cutting baby's fingernails. Baby's fingernails grow very fast, and new parents are often afraid to cut them. Sometimes babies are born with fingernails so long that they need to be cut right away to prevent them from scratching their faces. It is easiest to trim a baby's fingernails while baby is asleep. A baby's toenails do not seem to grow as fast. You may notice that your baby's toenails seem to be ingrown into the sides of his toes. Because a baby's toenails are soft and flexible, do not worry—ingrown toenails are seldom a problem in babies.

Bathing baby. In the first week or two before your baby's cord drops off, just give her a sponge bath. As soon as the cord is gone and the navel looks healed, you can start putting your baby into a tub bath. You need a warm, draft-free room, a basin of warm water, and a thick towel on which to place your baby. There are many types of baby tubs on the market, or you can simply use the kitchen sink which makes great pictures for the baby book and really tickles the fancy of other children. A washing tip: Wear a pair of old white gloves and rub a little mild baby soap on the wet glove. You have an instant wash cloth that automatically shapes itself to baby's body and reduces the slipperiness of bare hands on soapy skin. Also, place a towel in the bottom of the sink to prevent baby from slipping. When washing baby's face, just use water. Soap in the eyes can really hurt. Cotton-tipped applicators are handy for cleaning little crevices in and behind the outer ear, but never try to clean inside his ear canal.

Bathing is really play time; babies don't get dirty enough to need daily baths for cleanliness. Twice a week (especially in the winter) is enough bathing as long as the diaper area is washed every time there is a bowel movement.

Getting baby to enjoy bath time. Some babies protest their bath, while others enjoy it. A beautiful solution to bath-time protests is to take your baby into your bath with you. Get the water ready, a little cooler than you usually have it; then undress youself and undress your baby. Hold her close to you as you step into the water, and enjoy this beautiful skin-to-skin contact. If you are afraid of slipping with your baby, recline in the bath first and have someone else hand you your baby. If your baby still fusses upon entering the water in your arms, put him to your breast first and let him nurse until you slowly ease your way into the bath. This is a special way to enjoy mothering and bathing your baby.

Powders and oils are unnecessary, since your baby's skin is naturally rich in body oil. Too much soap robs baby's skin of these oils. Powders easily cake and build up in skin creases and can actually contribute to skin irritation and rashes. Oils may serve as a medium for the growth of harmful skin bacteria. Powders, if inhaled, may irritate baby's nasal and air passages. Scented oils and powders also camouflage the natural baby scent which mothers find irresistible.

Massaging baby. Babies love an oil massage. Undress your baby completely and sit on the floor with your baby on a thick towel on your outstretched legs. Use pure vegetable oil to lubricate your hands and gently massage baby's entire body. Even in the newborn period your baby's skin, arms, legs, and back are sturdy enough to accept a systematic, firm but gentle stroking. It is best to time an infant massage for just before your baby's usual fussy time of the day, usually late afternoon. A helpful reference for learning infant massage is *Infant Massage*, by Vimala Schneider (Bantam Books, 1989).

114

Purifying your infant's environment. Baby's nasal passages are very tiny. Also, newborns are obligate nose breathers, meaning that they need to breathe through their noses rather than their mouths. A newborn with a stuffed nose does not breathe through her mouth but rather struggles to get more air through her nose. The most common cause of nasal stuffiness is irritants in the environment. Cigarette smoke, perfumes, hair sprays, and aerosol fragrances are common nasal irritants. Crib toys such as fuzzy animals and other dust collectors can also cause nasal stuffiness. See Key 27 for tips on clearing baby's nose.

Regulating the temperature of your baby's environment. The smaller the baby, the more careful you need to be about changes in temperature. As a rule, babies may not adjust well to marked temperature swings for the first few weeks; premature babies and babies weighing less than five pounds may have immature temperature-regulating systems for the first few weeks, and especially need to be kept warm. Full-term healthy newborns, especially large ones weighing more than eight pounds, have the body fat and sufficiently mature temperature-regulating system to adapt easily to an environmental temperature comfortable to an adult. Room temperature of about 70° F. is adequate for a full-term, healthy baby.

Humidity is as important as the actual temperature. Relative humidity in the room helps maintain the constancy of the heat and keeps your baby's narrow nasal passages from drying out. A relative humidity of at least 50 percent is advisable. A dry climate or central heating may necessitate the use of a humidifier or vaporizer to maintain this level of humidity. Signs that the humidity in your baby's sleeping room is too low are persistently clogged nasal passages, sniffy breathing, and dry skin.

Dressing your baby. The way you dress your baby is a matter of culture and temperature. As a general guide, dress your baby in the same amount of clothing as you would wear for a given temperature and then add one more layer. Cotton clothing is preferable because it absorbs body moisture and allows air to circulate. Also, be sure the clothing is loose enough to allow your baby to move freely. Usually a sacque or kimono is adequate for a newborn in a warm climate; wrap the baby in a receiving blanket when it is cooler.

Taking baby outside. If you live in a climate where the indoor and outdoor temperatures are similar, then a full-term baby weighing more than eight pounds is able to go outside immediately after birth. By the time your baby weighs around eight pounds, he has enough body fat and his temperature-regulating system is mature enough to tolerate brief exposure to temperature swings, such as those experienced traveling from house to car and back. Babies less than six pounds may not tolerate marked changes in temperature well; therefore, it is necessary to maintain some consistency of temperature by traveling from a heated house to a heated car. It is wise to avoid unnecessary crowds for the first month, especially if baby is premature or has had some breathing problems at birth.

30

~~~~~~

INTRODUCING THE NEW BABY TO SIBLINGS

Children over three years of age usually welcome a new baby into the house with joy, realizing how much fun it will be to play with. Children under two, however, may not welcome a new baby with wide open arms. Although sibling rivalry is normal, there are ways of minimizing it.

Encourage your child to get acquainted with your baby before birth by "talking" to the new baby inside mommy. Let your child place his or her hand on the "bulge," feel the baby kick, and get the feeling that there is a real baby inside. By telling him this baby is just like he was when he was a baby, you help your child identify with the baby and you. Read picture books on how baby grows to your child. Picture books help clarify misconceptions; baby is not in mommy's *tummy*, he is in mommy's *uterus*.

Show your child baby pictures of herself when she was a tiny baby. Be sure to prepare your child for the time when you will go into the hospital. She will probably be more interested in what is going to happen to her while you are gone than what is going on in the hospital. Tell her where she is going and who will take care of her. Market the whole idea of separation from you not as a loss but as something special: "Grandma will read you some nice books and do special things with you." It is usually better to have a substitute parent take care of your child in your own home rather than have her cared for elsewhere. This helps alleviate her mounting suspicions that she is being displaced. Have the substitute caregiver hold to the child's routine as much as possible while you are gone. If a bedroom shuffle is needed to make room for the new baby, do this well in advance of the birth.

While you are in the hospital, communicate with your child often by phone. Bring him to the hospital often to see you and the new baby. After the birth, get your child involved with the care of the new baby. Involvement is the key to the very young child who has ambivalent feelings. Encourage him to be mommy and daddy's little helper, changing diapers and bathing the baby. The role of helper gradually should evolve into the role of teacher. Encourage the older child to teach the younger child. This will profit both of them. The older child will feel older and wiser as he "teaches" his little brother something. The older child may also become a source of developmental stimulation for the younger child. Using your older child as a teaching model is a real boost to his self-esteem and consequently may encourage desirable behavior towards the new baby.

Encourage your child to verbalize negative feelings. If she says, "I hate that baby," don't say, "No, you don't." If you deny her feelings, you are denying her right to feel emotions. It is better to express your understanding of these negative feelings and to pursue them and to turn them into more positive feelings. Allow your child much time and space to approve of the new baby.

Having siblings at the birth. If your hospital permits, and certainly if you deliver either at home or in a birthing center, the benefits of having siblings share the birth far outweigh the problems. In our family of seven, siblings have been present at the births of our last four babies. In our experience, children over three years of age appreciate the dignity of birth. If you choose to have siblings at the birth, have someone present at the birth whose sole purpose is to attend to the older siblings. The laboring mother should not be distracted from birthing her new baby by the disturbing behavior of the older children. Explain to the children what is going on during labor and, if they wish, allow them to watch the birthing process. For unforgettable memories, videotape the verbal and facial expressions of the siblings during the birth. We have noticed that a deep bonding occurs between the siblings and the new baby when they are present at birth. If siblings seem to be disturbed by the normal maternal noises, it may be wise either to explain them or to temporarily escort the children out of the birthing room.

Make your older child feel important, too. Well-meaning friends and relatives may make a great fuss over the new baby and shower him with a lot of gifts. Wise gift-bearing visitors will also bring gifts for your older child; in case they don't, have a few spare, wrapped gifts waiting in reserve.

Because the older child probably feels that she has lost a lot of mommy's prime time, father must take over giving the older child special time, so that the older child feels that what she has "lost" from mom she has gained from dad.

Wearing your baby in a baby sling lessens sibling rivalry. By wearing your new baby in a carrier, you have two hands free to do things with the older child. While you sit and nurse the baby in the carrier, you can be reading a book or playing with your older child. If some older children resent baby being in mom's arms all the time, encourage them to "wear" a doll or even a pet in their own homemade slings.

31

〰〰〰〰〰〰〰〰〰〰〰〰〰〰〰〰〰〰〰〰〰〰〰〰〰〰

INFANT STIMULATION

N ew parents frequently ask "How can we make our baby smarter?" Love for their babies and a desire to give their babies the best start make new mothers and fathers particularly vulnerable to the recent flurry of methods claiming to make for brighter babies. I wish to share with eager new parents the latest research on the benefits and pitfalls of these programs and to put infant stimulation in a healthy perspective for the sake of both babies and parents.

Dr. Susan Ludington, founder of the Infant Stimulation Education Association, defines the goal of what she calls "infant stim": "A well-rounded, well-balanced baby: One who is equally comfortable and confident in mental, motor, social, and emotional skills." Since babies don't come with directions, the following are practical and fun ways to help you and your baby achieve these goals.

Choose age and stage-appropriate toys. Classes and toys do not a super baby make. During the early months, parents are the baby's primary playmates; however, appropriate toys are a welcome addition to a baby's widening interest. The better infant stimulation classes teach parents to look at toys from a baby's point of view—to take into account what babies enjoy and are capable of doing at a given stage of development. For example, research has shown that in the first few months, babies relate best to contrasting stripes, dots, bulls' eyes and checkerboard patterns. For infant stimulation, then, black and white is in. Babies do not seem to show a preference for colors until after four months. Pastel colors, favored by designers, appear to be the least favorite of tiny babies. One of the most appropriate toys for a one-month-old I have ever seen is a black-and-white mobile needlepointed by a grandmother. A mobile play tip: Babies are more visually attentive when upright than when lying on their backs. If you want to stimulate your baby's visual development, instead of always having him lie prone gazing at dangling mobiles, sit him upright in an infant seat or on your lap or let him gaze over your shoulder; you will notice that he is more interested in objects for a longer time span.

Research shows that tiny babies relate best to objects that are round, soft, in contrasting dark and light, and ever changing. As you may have guessed, I have just described the human face—the familiar faces of mom and dad are still the most powerful infant stimulators. Because of babies' fascination with familiar faces, we have placed an 8 × 10 black-and-white picture of my wife and me along the sides of our baby's bassinet.

One basic principal of toy selection is called "contingency play": The reaction a baby gets from a toy should be contingent on the action of the baby. For example, kicking or batting a dangling mobile or shaking a rattle produces both movement and sound, so the baby soon learns cause and effect and develops a feeling of competency. Even babies as early as a month of age enjoy the reaction of seeing a mobile move as a result of their own kick. Another tip for infant stimulation: Change toys frequently. With the same old toys, babies, in infant-stimulation lingo, "habituate"; in plain language, they get bored.

Dialogue with your baby. During the early months, one of the most stimulating activities is talking and listening to your baby. "Dialoguing" with the baby fulfills all the four "R's" of infant stimulation: *R*hythm, *r*eciprocity, *r*epetition and *r*einforcement. Video analysis of mothers talking to their newborns shows that even a newborn baby moves his head in synchrony with his mother's speech. Mothers who have learned effective baby talk develop a reciprocity with their babies, described in Key 19. Although the newborn baby doesn't talk, the mother behaves as if the baby had responded. Mother and baby learn to take turns: Mother talks, baby listens. In later months baby babbles or gestures and mother listens. Mothers can also learn when *not* to talk to babies; for example, during feedings most babies want to get down to the business of sucking, rather than talking or listening. Both mother and baby develop the ability to hold each other's attention—one of the most important goals of infant stimulation; this ability to initiate a social exchange empowers the baby with a feeling of competence.

Researchers in infant stimulation advise that singing stimulates more of a baby's brain than simply talking. Did you know that when you sing to your baby, the lyrics impact the left half of the brain while the melody affects the right? If you play records, tapes, or FM stations on the radio, babies enjoy classical music which has slowly rising crescendos and decrescendos. Infants are usually bothered by rock music.

Individualize. Learn the facial gestures, tone of voice, holding patterns, and toys that are pleasing to your baby. Learn what your baby is capable of doing at each stage of development and what he or she seems to like or dislike. Make a list of baby's likes and dislikes. Rigid play programs deny your baby's individuality. A pediatrician's confession: As an index of mother-baby attachment during well-baby exams, I look for mothers who tell me more what baby likes than what he does. I encourage parents to pay attention to what the baby enjoys instead of what he can do; a baby still has plenty of time to make his measured debut into a performance-oriented society!

"Group therapy." I feel that one of the main benefits of infant stimulation classes, "play with baby classes," or "infant gym"—whatever name they go by in your community—is that parents and babies have fun together. If you want to develop your own infant stimulation course, information can be obtained by writing to the Infant Stimulation Education Association, Dr. Susan Ludington, Director, UCLA Medical Center, Factor 5-942, Los Angeles, CA 90024.

There is no proof that fancy toys make brighter babies. When toys and programs designed to enrich babies are evaluated, mother as playmate still comes out on top. In a keynote address at the annual meeting of the American Academy of Pediatrics a few years ago, Dr. Michael Lewis, director of child development at Rutgers University Medical School, discussed the effects of early infant stimulation on later outcome. The single most important factor in increasing a child's cognitive development was the responsiveness of the mother to the cues of her infant. Few pediatricians involved in child development were surprised to hear this. Researchers in infant development are realizing that when parents and babies spend more time doing things together, the baby also develops the parents. The more you interact with your baby, the more you know and appreciate your infant's capabilities and preferences at each stage of development. Encouraging and stimulating your infant helps you achieve what I feel are the three basic goals of early parenting: to know your baby, to help your baby feel right, and to enjoy your baby.

32

∿∿

PARENTING THE HOSPITALIZED NEWBORN

Newborn intensive-care units have improved the quantity and quality of life for sick and premature babies. Nonetheless, an unfortunate consequence of these units is the separation of sick newborns from their mothers during a very separation-sensitive period. The mother who delivers a premature baby is deprived of the pregnancy feelings of preparedness and nesting that occurs later in the third trimester. Instead of showering a mother with congratulations for delivering a full-term, healthy baby, people focus their attention on the baby. What is usually a joyous event becomes a crisis, and the mother may experience normal feelings of failure for being unable to carry the baby to term. If the newborn is very premature or very sick, parents may doubt the baby's survival and, to prepare themselves for the possibility of baby's death, may unconsciously detach themselves from the baby. What should be a period of attachment becomes a period of detachment; what should be a period of joy may become a period of grieving. Because of their early detachment from baby during a sensitive period, some parents may have difficulty reattaching to the baby and getting into parenting even after the baby is well and comes home from the hospital.

Involvement in your baby's care is the key to soothing the pain of separation. The advantage of delivering your baby in a hospital that has a newborn intensive-care unit is that you can still have a bonding relationship with your newborn; this early bonding will be delayed if your baby must be transferred to another hospital and you and your baby are no longer within touching and seeing distance of each other. Technology can never replace the parents; the care of a sick and hospitalized newborn is a team approach, and parents are a very important part of the medical team. As a former director of a university hospital newborn nursery, I encourage parents to sit "incubatorside," to stroke and caress their babies, to attempt eye-to-eye contact, and to talk to their babies. I have noticed that prematures who are stroked by their parents have fewer "stop-breathing" episodes and show a faster weight gain. Breastfeeding your hospitalized infant is another way to stay involved. Even if your baby is too premature to suck vigorously at your breast, your pumped breast milk contributes vital nutrients. Premature babies need more proteins and calories for "catch-up" growth. It has recently been discovered that the milk of mothers who deliver premature babies is higher in proteins and calories—another example of how mother's milk adapts to foster the survival of her newborn.

Hospitalized newborns often become very agitated and cry a lot. This excess crying wastes a lot of energy that they need to grow and heal. Babies who are held and nursed cry less and are able to direct this energy into their healing. Even a baby a few days old can get used to her parents' presence and absence. Parents in my practice often leave tape recordings of their voices and have the tapes played to their babies when they themselves cannot be there. Anything that you can do to keep in touch with your hospitalized infant helps both you and your baby.

Kangaroo care. A new method of care for preterm infants has become very popular in Europe and is getting increasing recognition in the United States. Called kangaroo care, an affectionate term derived from the method's similarity to the way the preterm infant is cared for in the kangaroo's pouch; the method requires the mother to hold her diaper-clad infant underneath her clothing, placing the baby tummy to tummy, skin to skin between or on her breasts. The skin-to-skin contact, the mother's warmth, and the vestibular stimulation of rocking and walking with the baby have shown medical benefits. Infants cared for with this method have shown stable temperatures, fewer stop-breathing episodes, and better weight gain. Because these infants spend more time in the optimal behavioral state of quiet alertness followed by deep sleep, they waste less energy crying and can concentrate on healing and growing. Even infants born as early as 28 weeks of gestation have been helped by kangaroo care. This blending of newborn intensive care and natural mothering is simply good common sense. As one well-coping mother of a very premature baby stated, "He's still in my womb, but now I can watch him grow." Both she and her baby adapted well to the system of kangaroo care. Spend as many hours as you can at the bedside of your hospitalized baby, becoming knowledgeable about the details of your infant's care and participating as much as you can in the hands-on care of your baby. Incidentally, studies have failed to show any increase in the rate of infection for hospitalized babies whose parents who are actively involved in their care.

The exciting results coming out of newborn intensive-care units that are practicing kangaroo care are validating the medical importance of parental involvement in the care of the premature and hospitalized infant.

33

‸‸‸

RECOGNIZING WHEN YOUR NEWBORN IS SERIOUSLY ILL

T he key to recognizing the sick newborn is to become familiar with the well newborn. Become familiar with your newborn's state of health—her breathing patterns, heart rate, skin color, the intensity of her suck, the gaze of her eyes, the strength of her muscle tone, her eating patterns, and her sleeping patterns.

When a newborn is seriously ill, many or all of these patterns change noticeably. A persistent and increasing change in many of your baby's normal behaviors and normal appearance over a period of a day or two should alert you to seek medical attention. The following are specific signs and symptoms that require prompt medical attention.

1. Increasing lethargy, drowsiness, diminishing responsiveness, and an overall limp feeling and appearance. Normally tiny infants are bright-eyed and responsive to their environment. Their muscle tone is strong and tight, and their arms and legs spring back toward their body when you lift them. You may notice a marked difference in her usual cry as part of lethargy—it may be either very high-pitched or very weak.

2. Persistent paleness of the skin and/or blueness of the lips. When a baby is well, her circulation

is well and she has a normal tone to her cheeks and skin.

3. Decreasing interest in feedings and diminished intensity of sucking lasting over eight hours. It is normal for a baby to show an occasional disinterest in feedings and an occasional weak suck. A persistent change in normal feeding patterns should be cause for concern. Babies normally suck with great gusto, feed frequently every two to four hours, and enjoy sucking from breast or bottle from 10 to 20 minutes at a time. A sick baby lacks the energy to do this.

4. Persistent rapid breathing (greater than 60 breaths per minute) during sleep and lasting for an hour or more or labored respirations (the chest goes in and out deeply as if baby is gasping for air). It is normal for a newborn to breathe very fast and very shallowly, especially while awake or upset. An occasional short period of rapid breathing as an isolated finding, with none of the other warning signs present, may be normal.

5. Green vomiting and/or watery green diarrhea resulting in obvious weight loss and signs of dehydration (dry diapers, dry eyes, dry mouth, and loose skin).

6. A temperature greater than 101° F rectally that lasts more than eight hours. Newborns normally do not run fevers, although an occasional temperature of 99 to 100° after crying or at the end of a busy day may not be abnormal if your baby is generally well. Before you leave the hospital or at your baby's first well-baby checkup, ask the nurse to show you how to take your baby's rectal

temperature and how to read the thermometer accurately. Get accustomed to kissing your baby's forehead and feeling her normal temperature. In case you missed this lesson, here's how to take your baby's temperature. First, use a rectal thermometer—it is the easiest and most accurate in a newborn. The only difference between rectal and oral thermometers is in the tip; the rectal thermometer is short and stubby to prevent injury to the rectum, while the tip of the oral thermometer is long and thin. To take your newborn's rectal temperature, shake down the thermometer (over a bed or rug in case you drop it). Grease the bulb end with petroleum jelly. Lay your baby face down across your lap, and gently insert the thermometer bulb about one inch into the rectum. Don't force it. Allow the thermometer to seek its own path. Hold the thermometer between your index and middle fingers with the palm of your hand and your fingers grasping your baby's buttocks. This way you can hold the thermometer and keep your baby from moving. Never leave your baby alone with the thermometer in place. Try to keep the thermometer in place for three minutes. If your baby is struggling, one minute may be long enough to get the reading within a degree of the true temperature. Take your baby's temperature when she is quiet. Crying vigorously may slightly elevate your baby's normal temperature.

If you closely attach to your newborn as if she is part of you, you will know her so well that you will judge her state of health by the way she looks, feels, and acts. Any departure from her normal state will alert you to a possible illness.

34

POSTPARTUM DEPRESSION

The arrival of a new baby into the family can turn your previously settled and predictable lifestyle upside down for a while. As the euphoria of giving birth begins to wear off, you will probably experience some emotional highs, coupled with lows ranging from a slight degree of after-baby blues to major postpartum depression. Most women experience some degree of temporary baby blues within a week or two after giving birth, probably because as they adjust to becoming a parent, a low naturally follows a high. Most women experience many of the following signs and symptoms to varying degrees: fatigue; confused thoughts and difficulty concentrating; episodes of crying, anxiety, and fear; loss of appetite; periods of nervousness and tension; insomnia; worry about physical appearance and unattractiveness, with diminishing desire to groom yourself; feelings of failure and panic; tendency to "make mountains out of mole hills," negative feelings toward husband; and fear of going crazy.

In addition to these feelings, you may experience doubt about your mothering abilities and frustration about your apparent lack of success. These feelings may lead to despair, and occasional negative feelings toward your baby, followed in turn by guilt for having them. Do not feel you are alone. Most postpartum mothers experience these feelings. Most postpartum adjustment difficulties are caused by too many changes too fast; depression is your body's signal that you have exceeded your physical and psychological ability to adapt to these changes.

Many women try to resume their previous busy lifestyle too fast. Other mothers, unprepared for the immense time and energy a new baby takes, try to be all things to all people, and it just doesn't work. It is important to recognize these feelings early and consider them your body's signal that you have exceeded your ability to cope and that changes need to be made.

Your changing body chemistry, especially your hormones, also contribute to postpartum blues. Changing body chemistry brings with it changing moods and feelings. You will recognize early on that babies don't sleep through the night; sleep deprivation is a contributing factor to postpartum depression.

Identity problems can also contribute to postpartum blues. This is particularly true of a woman who has had an exciting career outside the home from which she received much status and affirmation. A new mother may feel that she is always known in relation to someone else: "I'm Mary's mother, I'm John's wife, but what happened to me as a person?" At no other time in a married couple's life do so many changes occur so fast as in the immediate postpartum period—changes in lifestyles, role changes for husband and wife, disrupted routines, disrupted sleep patterns, and changes in economic status. Coping with these changes helps mature new parents.

There are steps you can take to prevent or alleviate postpartum depression. Some suggestions are:

1. Join a support group, either through the La Leche League or your childbirth class.
2. Room in with your baby after birth.

3. Enjoy your maternity leave. Don't try to return to your previous lifestyle and other commitments too soon.

4. Take a few hours each week to do something just for you—an exercise class, a massage, a walk in the park, shopping, whatever pleases you. Pamper yourself—you deserve it.

5. Entertain visitors only when you wish to. You should have no social obligations except to yourself, your baby, and your husband.

6. Exercise. Get at least a half hour of sustained exercise each day, even if it is simply walking in the park with your baby in a carrier.

7. Honor your husband with his share of household chores. An untidy nest often causes an upset mother. My own wife is bothered by one dirty dish in the postpartum period, even though normally a whole pile of dirty dishes doesn't upset her. If friends ask what you need say, "Bring over supper and clean my house."

8. Eat well, even if you have to sometimes force yourself to eat.

9. Keep yourself physically attractive. Most mothers feel good when they look good.

10. Finally, breastfeed your baby as often as you can, taking advantage of the relaxing effects of the breastfeeding hormones. Sleep when your baby sleeps. During baby's sleep time is not the time to "get something done." There is nothing else so important in the postpartum period as caring for your baby—and yourself.

35

~~~~~~

PARENTING THE ADOPTED NEWBORN

M ost adopting couples become parents suddenly and with very little preparation or advance notice. I am amazed how quickly adopting couples bond with the newborn even without the hormonal changes that biological mothers have. It seems that the overwhelming desire to parent a baby can be strong.

To get the right start with your adopted newborn, be involved with the birth. If possible, try to hold your baby immediately after birth and be the first persons to interact with the baby. Before the birth of the baby, let the attending medical personnel know that you want to have some private time with your baby immediately after birth. Within an hour after birth babies have around a ten- to twenty-minute period of quiet alertness when they are very wide-eyed and receptive to interaction with their caregivers. These caregivers should be you.

Be involved in the early feedings. Under medical supervision, hold and feed your baby during the early days in the hospital. Feeding is very much of a social interaction with a newborn and should be done by you. While it's unlikely you will be able to make all the feedings, work out a feeding schedule with the nursery nurses and attend as many as you can.

One of the fascinating innovations in helping adoptive parents bond with the newborn is a new technique for breast-feeding the adopted baby. While it may initially surprise many mothers, adopting mothers can breastfeed. This is done under supervision with a trained lactation consultant and the use of a supplemental nursing system (SNS), an ingenious device consisting of a flexible plastic bottle that hangs around your neck and rests between your breasts. A tiny polyethylene tube from inside the bottle is taped onto your breasts and fits approximately a half inch over your nipple. The bottle is filled with formula. When your newborn sucks from your nipple, she sucks the milk from the bottle through the tubing. The SNS benefits baby and mother. Baby thinks the milk is coming from the mother, enhancing the mother-infant bond. In addition, the sucking of your baby on your nipple over a period of time releases mothering hormones that give the adopting mother the benefits of the same hormones biological mothers have. Over a period of approximately six weeks, adopting mothers even begin producing some of their own milk. We have had about five years of experience in teaching adopting mothers how to breastfeed. The least important factor in this beautiful relationship is how much milk the adopting mother produces; we do not focus on this but emphasize the bonding interaction and hormonal stimulation that adopted nursing provides.

If you choose not to "breastfeed" your adopted baby, hormonal stimulation and a close bond with your newborn can be achieved by a great deal of skin-to-skin contact and interaction with your baby. One of the most important ways of achieving this is to practice the style of wearing your baby as described in Key 23.

36

~~~~~~

PARENTING THE HANDICAPPED NEWBORN

In parenting seminars, I have often commented, "Nothing matures a person like parenting a bunch of kids." This is especially true of mothering or fathering an infant with special needs. Our seventh child, Stephen, has Down Syndrome and has special needs requiring a special kind of parenting. As we parented Stephen we realized a very important principal of parenting—the need level concept, discussed in Key 21. Every child has a certain level of need, every parent a certain level of giving. A child with high needs requires high giving, sometimes causing parents to feel "gived out." Because a high-need child requires a high level of parent giving, parents naturally develop a higher level of parenting skills; they grow together. This principal of mutual giving reaches its peak with special children. Stephen is really bringing out the best in us. As one mother in my practice wrote to us, "Stephen will add to your lives flashes of color that you never knew life could lack—wait and see." How true this has turned out to be!

Become very involved with and knowledgeable about your baby's special problem. Knowledge of a problem facilitates acceptance of the problem. The more you understand your baby's special needs, the better your skills will be in developing a special parenting style to meet these needs. Ask your doctor to provide you with the most accurate reading material available on the subject of your child's special problem. Impress upon your health-care providers your need to know, emphasizing that you can handle specifics.

Don't compare babies. It is counterproductive and serves only to fuel the anger you may already have. One of the most important lessons we have learned in dealing with a special child is to value this child, not in relation to other children as the standard but because of his or her own unique characteristics. Dwelling on what the child is "missing" can be very upsetting.

The word "handicapped" is misleading; we are all handicapped to some extent. I have never seen a "handicapped" child who has not developed other qualities, both emotional and physical, to compensate for his or her special problem. It is these qualities that give the child uniqueness and value. Appreciate them and learn from them.

Seek support groups with caring people who lift your spirits when you are down. You will find that many of your feelings, such as anger and disappointment, are shared with countless numbers of others who have, to various degrees, handled them and grappled with the unanswerable question, "Why did this happen?" You will discover your feelings are very normal. Most county health agencies have a list of support groups for just about any type of condition.

To friends of parents who have had a handicapped newborn, let me offer the following advice. You will naturally be uneasy about what to say to the parents. Any child who is outside of the "normal" naturally makes us uneasy, but it is handling the special problems, not the usual or "normal," that make us grow. Be uplifting; depending on the type of problem, approach the new parents with a congratulatory spirit, not with sympathy. As an example, I recently attended the birth of a Down Syndrome baby, the first child born to a young couple. The grandparents on both sides and friends were in the waiting room. When I went out to speak to the grandparents, the atmosphere was more like a wake than a birth. Well-meaning but inappropriate comments such as, "Well, at least he can work at a fast-food restaurant," were made.

It helps to focus comments on the fact that this baby is first a person, one who also has some problems. Address the child by name, look for some special features that are pleasant to talk about, and use caring statements such as the one quoted to us above. Remember, the parents are equally uncomfortable about what to say to their own friends, and they catch your spirit. Approaching their baby with an uplifting tone gives more value to their baby.

Parents, surviving and thriving with a special needs baby requires a team approach. You are very valuable members of this team.

37

SINGLE MOTHERING THE NEWBORN

T he plight of the single mother is one of our most difficult social problems. Single-parent households constitute the fastest growing category of all family units. Whether you are a single mother by choice or because of divorce or the death of your husband, I offer the following survival keys.

Choose the right support. Mothers, especially single mothers, are never completely prepared for how parenting a newborn completely turns their life upside down for a while. It is nearly impossible to have enough energy to carry on your own life and parent a newborn alone. You need understanding and help. Try to find a single-parents support group in your community, with mothers who are in similar situations and who can offer you advice from their own experience. If your parents are able and willing to help, it may be necessary for financial and support reasons to move in with them for a while. Most large churches have single parents groups noted for their compassionate understanding of the difficulties of being a single mother; in these support groups you will meet other persons who can substitute-parent for you later on, to give you a break for yourself or perhaps to babysit should you return to work. Avoid nonsupportive persons or accusatory groups who give you the message that you shouldn't be in this situation in the first place. This is counterproductive.

Financial considerations. While financial circumstances vary greatly among single parents, there are a few general considerations. Plan ahead. Before your baby is born, try to save as much money as you can from your prenatal employment in order to delay returning to work as long as possible. This gives you time with your baby, time that both of you need in order to get to know each other. Nearly all states have programs that pay for medical care for the single mother and her baby when necessary. Usually the social worker in the hospital where you deliver your baby can make you aware of these programs and get you the necessary application forms even before the birth.

The federal government provides free food for both mother and baby through the Women, Infants, and Children (WIC) program. You may also be eligible for a housing allowance or a monthly income from Aid to Dependent Children (ADC). Do not feel belittled at having to accept welfare programs. You are entitled to them, as is your baby. Society regards infants and children as the most valuable of natural resources, and it is only right that society is willing to pay for them.

Choose the style of mothering that works for you, one in which you feel right. For single mothers, as for all parents, I highly recommend the attachment style of parenting (See Key 1). This style of parenting develops a mother's own intuition and gives you the boost of the natural mothering hormone that you are going to need to persevere during these trying times. Because you may have to be away from your baby later on to work, you may not be able to practice all of the elements of this style of parenting all the time. However, during your maternity leave in your baby's newborn period, you are able to practice all of these attachment styles and then gradually work some of them into your later lifestyle.

Single mothers are particularly vulnerable to outside advice from well-meaning friends and relatives who offer you guidance on taking care of your baby. Yours is a special situation that requires a special kind of mothering—do what works for you.

Choosing the right job is especially important for single parents, because you will later need this source of self-esteem to thrive both as a person and as a parent. If you have to work for financial reasons, as nearly all single mothers do, choose a job that builds your self-esteem and has a possibility of future advancement. Feeling fulfilled as a person is likely to carry over to your value as a mother. I grew up in a single-parent household from early infancy on, and to this day I remember one major fact about our situation: I have very warm feelings toward my mother, who did the very best she could in a less than ideal situation. Try to choose either a business you can conduct from home or one that allows you to take your baby with you to work. Another option is to seek employment with on-site day care so that you can spend as much time with your baby as possible. Don't try to be both a mother and a father to your baby—you aren't and you can't be. In the newborn period, a baby needs mothering; worry about male influence later.

38

~~~~~~

TRAVELING WITH YOUR NEWBORN

Newborns are very portable; in fact, the first few months are probably the easiest age to travel with babies. A little planning and attention to some safety factors can help assure that your trip is safe and successful.

Traveling by car. The first "trip" for a newborn is usually the trip home from the hospital. So that your first ride can be a safe ride, many hospitals either give, lend, or sell you an infant car seat for your newborn. Be mindful of the following criteria in selecting a safe car seat for your newborn: Car seats for newborns are designed to face backward so that the infant's back faces the front of the car and reclines at a 45° angle. The car seat is secured so that most of the forward force of a collision is transmitted to the seatbelt holding the seat. The rear-facing, semi-upright position allows the remaining force to be evenly distributed along baby's back, bones, and muscles. A safety harness secures the baby in the seat.

There are two types of car seats for newborns: tublike and convertible. The tublike seat is simple, lightweight, and less expensive than the convertible and can be used to transport a sleeping baby outside the car. The convertible type of carseat can be turned forward when baby weighs more than 20 pounds and can be used for the next couple of years until the child is large enough for a booster seat or a lap belt. Convertible seats are heavier and more expensive, but they eliminate the need to buy a second car seat when your child is older (about six months).

I cannot overemphasize the importance of securing your infant safely in an approved car seat every time you travel in a car. I have seen tragic results from removing an infant from a car seat in order to comfort her or from not placing the infant in the car seat because "we are only traveling a few blocks." Fortunately, most states now have laws requiring the use of safety seats and seatbelts.

While the safest place in the car is the center of the rear seat, I find that mothers are often distracted while driving if their infant is not within reach. If you are the driver and you find yourself constantly looking in the rear view mirror or turning around to observe your baby, it is probably best to place your baby next to you in the front seat in an approved car seat. If you are a passenger in the car and someone else is driving, it is best to sit in the back seat with your baby in a car seat in the center of the rear seat. Avoid the tendency to take your baby out of the car seat when she is crying. Instead, when your baby starts crying, lean over and breast-feed her (while she is still in the car seat), and you have one of the most ingenious crystoppers for car travel. Prepare your husband for what you are doing beforehand. The first time I saw the technique was during one of our car trips when, shortly after our baby started crying, I looked in the rear view mirror and saw a breast coming from one side of the mirror and a baby's head from the other, the two meeting in the midline and immediate silence. With a little bit of practice, this nursing technique can be mastered without either passenger being unstrapped.

Nothing upsets a driver like a crying baby. If you are driving with your baby in the car and find yourself becoming increasingly agitated, it is best to stop, comfort your baby, and then proceed with your trip.

Infant carriers make traveling easier for parents and for baby. Choose a sling-like carrier, and wear your baby wherever you go. This type of carrier keeps baby safely contained in busy crowds and protects against cigarette burns, things falling on baby, and baby snatching. A sling carrier also allows for discreet nursing in public. (See Key 23 for pointers on selecting a baby carrier.)

Traveling by air. When traveling by air with an infant, request a seat with a lot of leg room. The change in air pressure may produce ear pain in tiny babies; to lessen the pain, give your baby a breast or a bottle, especially during landing. If your baby is sleeping as the plane is descending, wake her up and nurse her (this is the only time I ever advise waking a sleeping baby). While baby is asleep the eustachian tubes do not function normally to equalize air pressure; nursing your baby helps alleviate the ear pain while the plane is landing.

Your newborn's travel kit. The following items should be part of your diaper bag or travel kit:
- Extra diapers, cloth and/or disposables
- Salt water nose drops and a nasal aspirator
- Sling-type baby carrier
- Sacque or kimono outfits
- Sleepers
- Diaper wipes
- Extra diaper pins
- Booties
- Sun hat (if traveling to a warm, sunny climate)
- Zinc oxide diaper cream

- Undershirts
- Extra clothing, depending and length of trip and climate

It is usually safe to travel with the newborn if baby's weight is over eight pounds, if his respirations are stable, and if baby is generally well. It is wise to check with your doctor for advice on when it is safe to travel with your particular baby. If you live in a warm, moderate climate and you are traveling to a similar climate, travel is quite safe in the newborn period; traveling from a warm climate to a much colder one is much more difficult for a baby to adjust to and requires much warmer clothing and greater vigilance to prevent baby getting cold. Traveling from a heated home to a heated car back into a heated home is safe. Newborns do not tolerate extremes of temperature changes well and are also dependent on humidity for comfortable breathing. Traveling to a vacation spot (such as a ski chalet heated by electric baseboard heat) with the newborn is not advisable, and a vaporizer or humidifier may be necessary in stuffy centrally-heated hotel rooms to prevent the dry air clogging baby's nasal passages.

Some babies may fuss a bit more during travel, mainly because of the upset in regular routines and all the commotion with admiring relatives playing pass-the-baby. In my experience, the main factor that upsets babies during travel is the fatigue of the mother. Trying to do too much for too many people during travel diverts your energy from your newborn—the person who most needs you. This is why it is unwise to plan to make the rounds of the family or to plan cross-country trips until after the newborn period unless absolutely necessary.

In general, newborns travel well and easily adapt to changing environments. "Home" to a tiny baby is where mother is.

39

RETURNING TO WORK

If you choose to or have to return to work immediately after the newborn period, consider the following tips on working and mothering. First, before your baby's birth and in the first few weeks afterwards, temporarily "forget" that you are returning to work. I have found that many mothers who wrestle with ambivalent feelings about returning to work handle these feelings by subconsciously not getting as close to their babies or enjoying them as much as they can. This distancing results from fear that otherwise they will find it extremely difficult to leave their infants. Enjoy your time as a full-time mother and don't spend your time worrying about when you have to return to work.

There are some necessary preparations that make returning to work easier on both you and your baby. Continue breastfeeding even after returning to work; mothers in my practice who have continued part-time breastfeeding have found making the transition from home to work much easier because they continue this special bond with their baby. Purchase a battery-operated portable breast pump, and take breaks at work to pump your milk at least every three hours. Incidentally, you have the legal right to time off to pump your milk. Store the milk in a clean bottle in a refrigerator, and either freeze it for future use or take it home for the babysitter to use the following day.

Breastfeed your baby before you leave for work in the morning, as soon as you return home in the evening, and as frequently as possible on weekends and holidays. The "happy departure" nursing in the morning and the "happy reunion" nursing in the evening are usually the most pleasant.

Encourage your substitute caregiver not to feed your baby within an hour of when you're expected home. As soon as you return home, take the phone off the hook, turn on some soothing music, put your feet up, and nurse. Many mothers find that breastfeeding their baby as soon as they return home helps them unwind from a hectic day's work, probably because of the relaxing effect of the hormone prolactin.

Share sleep with your baby. Many mothers report that when they return to work, their babies begin to wake up frequently at night. The mothers are therefore so tired that they find it difficult to work the next day. The reason for this is that babies often tune out the babysitter during the day and become frequent nightfeeders as a way of being with mother. This situation is alleviated by allowing your baby to sleep next to you so that neither you nor your baby fully awakens during feeding and your sleep is less disturbed. The night feeding also allows your milk supply to continue.

Encourage or, better yet, insist that your husband do his share of the household chores. If you are going to continue breastfeeding and working, you will need domestic help.

Think "baby" while at work. Many mothers surround themselves with pictures of their babies while at the office. Having a picture (both actual and mental) of your baby while you are using a breast pump helps activate your milk-producing hormones.

Be prepared for temporary adjustment nuisances, such as breast engorgement and leaking. These discomforts subside within a few weeks as your body adjusts to your new breastfeeding routine.

146

Choose a substitute caregiver who intuitively shares your style of mothering. Insist that she give your baby a nurturant response to cries, carry your baby a lot, and interact with your baby. She is not a babysitter, she is a substitute mother. Tell her how you want your baby mothered.

Exciting changes are occurring to incorporate mothering into the marketplace. Mothers in my practice have found ingenious ways to spend a lot of time with their baby while pursuing an outside career and earning a second income. Among the options are home-run businesses, flex-time (flexible working hours according to the moods and needs of your baby), job sharing (two or more mothers dividing one full-time job) and taking their babies to work with them. At this writing, two of my office nurses have recently had babies and are now wearing them around the office while they perform their work. Bargain with your employer about flexible working hours and incorporating your mothering into your work. Employers find mothers who merge parenting and working do a better job since they're so happy to find a working environment that recognizes their need to both mother and work and relieves their anxieties about how their babies are faring without them.

40

~~~~~~

MARRIAGE ADJUSTMENTS TO THE NEW BABY

Remember those uninterrupted candlelight dinners for two? Now they are dinners for three and likely to be interrupted. New parents-to-be are so ecstatic at the thought of having a baby that they do not want to hear of the stresses and strains the baby will impose on their lifestyle. During the first month, though, reality hits. You finally realize that this little newborn whom you love so deeply can turn your previously settled and predictable world completely upside down for a while, and you experience temporarily upsetting changes in your sleep patterns, meal patterns, and intimate time together. Here is what to expect and how to cope.

The main change in your married life is that you will have less time and energy for each other. This is a necessary fact of new-parent life. Your family's very important third person, while little in size, is big on demands and usually drains from a new mother every bit of her extra energy. A wise mother prepares for this by temporarily shelving unnecessary energy demands and focusing on her baby, herself, and her family. Because of the excess energy demands and especially the upset sleep schedules (or lack of sleep), it is usual for a new mother to be very tired and on edge during the first month. She may seem to have a short fuse and snap at her husband over seemingly insignificant things.

The increased energy demands of the new baby drain the new mother, so that she has little time left for anything else, especially sex. Mothers of particularly draining babies have confided in me the following during the early months after birth: "I feel touched out"; "I feel all used up." Fathers have also confided, "All she does is nurse; I feel left out." These father feelings are quite usual and normal; fathers feel left out of the inner circle of mother-infant attachment, and it is easy to conclude that your wife has lost interest in you. This is seldom the case. Perhaps this normal phenomenon of new family life is easier described if you understand the normal changes that go on in a woman after she gives birth and what I call the seasons of a marriage.

Prior to birth a woman has two sets of hormones, mothering hormones and sexual hormones. Prior to birth the level of her sexual hormones is higher than that of her mothering hormones, and her desire to mate may be greater than her desire to mother. After birth, the reverse occurs. Her mothering hormones dominate her sexual hormones so that her need to mother is greater than her need to mate. This, I feel, is a natural biological phenomenon with survival benefit for the young of the species. This temporary hormonal reversal represents a temporary season of the marriage—a season to parent. This means not that your wife has lost interest in you but that energies that were previously directed toward you are now temporarily diverted toward your baby. After weaning or in later months of infant care, the mother's hormones resettle somewhat, and her sexual energies return.

While mother's hormones change after birth, it is important for women to remember that men's hormones do not.

As you expect your husband to be sensitive to your changes, you need to be mindful of his needs. For a more in-depth description of sexuality changes and how to rekindle the sexual fire, see Barron's *Keys to Becoming a Father.*

The adjustment to life after birth is much easier if the couple sits down and discusses these changes, anticipates problems, and does a bit of preventive medicine. It took us several children to realize the importance of keeping the marriage flame burning through those exhausting early months of parenting. We have always enjoyed a dinner for two at least once a week. Our older children have learned to respect this time out; sometimes they even make a game out of it and act like our waiters. We continue the custom even when there is a newborn in the house, simply making it a dinner for three. Baby sleeps in a little cradle or bassinet right next to our dining table and we enjoy our dinner for two, being mindful of the little third person's presence. Sometimes we are interrupted, sometimes we are not.

It helps for husband and wife to share their feelings honestly. If you as mother are giving out and find too many demands on your energy, say so. Ask for help—ask your husband to help more around the house or hire some help. Fathers, take a paternity leave if you can or at least try when you are home to be very sensitive to the increasing needs of your wife. Define and take over whatever household chores drain energy from your wife. Fathers are often not very good at anticipating what their wives need, and mothers are often reluctant to ask for help. Sensitivity to each other's needs is the key to life with a new baby.

Your newborn is a baby a very short time. Remember, this high-maintenance stage will soon pass. Yes, there is marriage after birth.

QUESTIONS AND ANSWERS

Q. We would like to have our baby circumcised but don't want to put him through the pain. I have heard about using a local anesthetic. Is this possible?

Yes. It is a myth that newborns do not feel pain during circumcision. Studies comparing the physiologic effects of circumcision on anesthetized and unanesthetized babies show the following: Babies who did not receive a local anesthetic cried more, developed higher heart rates, had higher levels of stress hormones, showed a drop in blood oxygen, and generally seemed more stressed. The procedure you refer to is called a dorsal penile nerve block, meaning that a small amount of xylocaine is injected just beneath the skin on both sides of the penis to numb the skin where the incision is made. I have personally used this technique on several hundred babies and have experienced no complications. If your doctor is unaware of this technique, the procedure is described in the *Journal of Pediatrics*, 1978, vol. 92, p. 998.

While the number of circumcisions in the United States is gradually diminishing, many parents still prefer to have their baby circumcised although they do not want to inflict pain. A local anesthetic alleviates much of the pain for the baby—and the parents.

Q. I have heard that laboring in water eases the pain of labor and delivery. Is this true?

Yes, laboring in water is less painful. Water birthing has been practiced in Russia and France for the past ten or twenty years. Only recently has this natural labor-saving technique been used in the United States. The reason water works is simple: A relaxed mother has a relaxed uterus, which leads to a more normal labor. The buoyancy of water enables the mother to labor in the most comfortable position because she can move easily, support her body, and better deal with the contractions. In addition, her muscles are less tense because they do not have to support her entire weight. As the mother relaxes, her stress hormones decrease and the natural birth-progressing hormones flow uninhibited. Birthing tubs (as these jacuzzi-like tubs are now called) are intended to ease the pain and improve the process of labor. Many women ultimately give birth in the water because of their reluctance to emerge from it in spite of their impending delivery. After studying the results achieved by competent obstetricians who encourage water labor and water birthing in their practices, I have concluded that over the next few years most hospitals will offer water labor to their obstetrical patients. In experienced hands, water labor is not just a passing fad but a growing reality. Any method that eases discomfort and improves the health of the mother and baby during labor must be taken seriously. My wife, Martha, experienced water labor with the birth of our seventh baby, Stephen. After trying all other comforting measures without relief, Martha got into the birthing tub. She relates, "Water made it possible for me to relax, and the pain melted away. For me, water labor was wonderful. When the birth was imminent, I got out of the tub and delivered in the birthing bed." For an in-depth discussion of the benefits, techniques, and safety of water birthing, see the *Journal of Nurse-Midwifery*, 1989, vol. 34, pp. 165–70.

Q. We are considering a home birth but are a little scared about this. Are home births safe?

Before you decide, do your homework carefully. The American Academy of Obstetricians and Gynecologists (AGOG) has taken a wise position on home births, stating that if couples are properly selected and the birth is properly attended, home birthing may be as safe as hospital birthing. However, because of the possibility of unanticipated obstetrical complications, the best choice for most couples is a home-like birthing environment in an LDR room in a birthing center or hospital. The following factors may influence your decision about a possible home birth: whether you have had previous uncomplicated deliveries, whether your current pregnancy has been uncomplicated, and whether your doctor anticipates a preterm delivery or unusual positioning (e.g., breach). If you have a normal obstetrical history and, most important, if you have selected a qualified birth attendant and have medical backup close by in case of an unanticipated complication, you may consider home birth. If you do choose home birth attended by a qualified midwife, it is wise to consult also with an obstetrician in case specialized services are needed during and/or after delivery. Remember, childbirth is a very important event; you want to do everything possible to increase your chance of having a healthy baby and a healthy mother.

Q. Our baby was just born two months prematurely. His breathing problems have now subsided, but the doctors say he will need to be in the hospital for at least a month in order to grow. I know he needs special care, but I feel left out as a mother. What can I do?

You are a very important and indispensable part of the medical team. Premature babies do need special care by a lot of medical personnel, and they need it for a long time. It is easy

153

for parents to feel left out of this inner circle. Here's how you can help care for your baby. First, realize that it is normal for you to distance yourself somewhat from your baby psychologically. Parents of premature babies often do this as a protective mechanism against the grief of possibly losing their baby. Since it seems that your baby is out of danger and will survive, it is time to assume your rightful role as his mother. Rent an electric breast pump and pump your milk. Breast milk is especially valuable for premature babies, both nutritionally and as a protection against infections to which preemies are especially susceptible. Spend as much time as possible cribside. Hold and rock your baby when he is able to be out of the incubator. If he has to be in the incubator, then sing to him, talk to him, and stroke his skin. One of the recent advances in caring for premature babies is called "kangaroo care," meaning that a baby off oxygen and intravenous support is wrapped securely around mother's chest and spends many hours each day in skin-to-skin contact with mother. The baby is kept warm and has the benefit of close contact with your breasts. Walk around the nursery with your baby packed closely against your body. Your warmth, your voice, your walking motion, all of which has become familir to the baby over the past seven months, and your skin-to-skin touch all benefit your baby in a way that medical personnel cannot. Studies have shown that this care-by-parent method helps prematures grow faster and leave the hospital sooner. One mother of a premature baby coped with the initial disappointment of prematurity by realizing, "Now I have the benefit of seeing our baby grow the final two months outside the womb." The more you participate in your baby's care, the more both of you will benefit. Encourage dad to get involved with baby care, too. Both of you are an important part of the medical team.

Q. I'm always changing diapers on our new baby. What are his bowel movements supposed to look like, and how often should I expect them to occur?

During the first few weeks, baby's stools change a lot. For the first few days, they are black, tarry, and sticky, because they contain a lot of the meconium that your baby had in his intestines while in the womb. Over the next few days, these stools become greenish brown in color and less sticky. Between one and two weeks, they take on a yellowish color and a pasty consistency. As the fat content of your milk increases, the stools of breastfeeding babies become yellow and seedy and develop a mustardlike consistency and a not-unpleasant aroma like buttermilk. Breast milk acts as a natural laxative, so you can expect a breastfed baby's stools to become frequent and soft. Formula-fed babies have firmer, darker, and more odorous stools. If you are using an iron-fortified formula, expect your baby's stools to have a greenish color from the iron. The number of stools a newborn baby has varies considerably. Some babies have a loose stool at every breastfeeding; you will sometimes hear the gurgly sound of a soft stool a few minutes into the feeding. Formula-fed babies usually have fewer stools than breastfed babies. You can also expect a change of stools with a change in diet. Changing formulas or adding solid foods to your baby's diet changes the color and consistency of the stools. As your baby gets older and eats more solids, expect the stools to become firmer, darker, and less frequent.

Q. We are about to have our first baby, and we are trying to decide what type of medical insurance would be best for our baby. Any suggestions?

The wise saying "You get what you pay for" is certainly true of medical insurance. At the present time the medical insurance industry is in a state of chaos, and new parents are left to flounder in a sea of uncertainty as to what type of insurance is best for their baby and for their budget. The best medical insurance for your baby is one that allows you your choice of doctors and choice of hospitals. You want to be able to choose a doctor who will grow with your baby from birth through adolescence, becoming like an extra member of the family and investing time and energy in your baby and your family. If you choose this unrestricted type of medical insurance, I also advise choosing a policy with a high deductible to obtain lower monthly premiums. If your baby is ill and needs to go into the hospital, you can usually pay the deductible off in small amounts over time, paying a total amount that is still lower than if you paid higher monthly premiums. Choose a reputable company that has been around for a long time and is likely to stay in business. The realistic fact of insurance life is that the best coverage is also the most expensive. If you are unable to choose the unrestricted type of medical insurance, you might consider a group plan offered by your place of employment. Be sure you are able to transfer out of this plan into an individual insurance policy without penalty in case your place of employment changes. There are numerous plans available, some of which have certain phrases like "preferred" attached. This usually means that you are restricted in your choice of doctors. If possible, avoid any plan that restricts your choice of doctors. Plans change, the doctors in the plans change, and your child will grow up being cared for by a series of anonymous doctors, none of whom make a long-term investment in your child.

Q. How much weight can I expect our new baby to gain over the next few weeks?

Newborns usually lose between five and eight percent of their birth weight (six to ten ounces) in the first week after birth.

The reason for this is that babies are born with extra fluid and fat to tide them over until their mother's milk can supply sufficient fluid and nutrition. Many factors affect the amount of weight a baby loses or gains. Large babies who have a lot of extra fluid tend to lose more weight than small babies. Weight loss during the first week is also affected by how soon the mother's milk increases; babies who room in with their mothers and breastfeed on cue lose less weight because the milk supply increases sooner and also because they get a higher-calorie milk. Babies who are often separated from their mothers during the first week or who are fed only according to a rigid schedule tend to lose more weight.

In addition to recording your baby's birth weight, you should record her weight upon discharge from the hospital; it will serve as an important reference point when your doctor checks your baby's weight one or two weeks later. Following the initial normal weight loss, a newborn should begin to gain weight around four to six days after birth. Breastfed babies usually show a slower weight gain than formula-fed babies during the first two weeks. Thereafter, breastfed babies and formula-fed babies show similar weight gains, both averaging about an ounce a day during the last two weeks of the first month. Most babies gain at least a pound to a pound and a half during the first month. In addition to feeding and care practices, your baby's body type may influence her weight gain. Ectomorphs (recognized by their lean and lanky appearance, long fingers, and long, narrow feet) show a slower gain in weight and a proportionately greater increase in height than do babies who are mesomorphic (of medium build) or endomorphic (short pugdy hands and feet and short, wide fingers and toes).

Q. Our newborn baby breathes so noisily. How can I tell if this is a cold?

A cold means an infection, and most of the noises that newborn babies make are not truly colds. Newborn babies have tiny nasal passages, and the lining of their noses is very susceptible to environmental irritants such as cigarette smoke, lint, and perfumes. Many times a stuffy nose is due to an environmental irritant, not a cold. Further, toward the end of the first month babies have a surge in saliva production, often making more than they can swallow. The excess saliva collects in the back of the throat, producing a gurgly sound. When you place your hand on your baby's chest or back, you may feel a rattle that you think is coming from his chest. What you are really feeling is the air vibrating the pooled saliva in the back of your baby's throat. These sounds and vibrations are transmitted throughout the chest but are not coming from within the chest. This is not truly a cold, and no medicine is necessary. Your baby will not choke on these secretions even though the noise he produces may be worrisome to you. With time he will learn to swallow the excess saliva, and the normal chest rattles will diminish. The saliva noises usually lessen when your baby falls asleep because babies produce less saliva when they sleep. On the other hand, your baby may well have an infection-type cold if the discharge from his nose begins as clear and watery and progresses to thick, yellow, and clotted, if his behavior goes from happy to cranky, if he seems less interested in feeding; and if he awakens more often. Persistent fever (over 101 for more than eight hours) should definitely be reported to your doctor. Fever in a newborn is much more serious a sign than in an older infant.

Q. Our newborn's bones seem to crackle a lot when we move him. Is this normal?

Yes. The joints of tiny babies are composed of many tiny bones held loosely together by very stretchy ligaments. The crackles you hear are these tiny moving parts sliding on each other during limb movement. These joint noises are common and normal and usually subside toward the end of the first year. Babies really are not fragile, and you don't have to worry about these noises. Like most of the normal but worrisome noises of infancy, these too will disappear.

Q. How often should we bathe our newborn, and what type of soap should we use?

Newborns bring out the mother-cat instinct; they are usually washed too much. Bathing is really play time; babies do not get dirty enough to need a daily bath. For busy parents, this is good news. Twice a week is enough bathing, provided you wash your baby's diaper area every time there is a bowel movement. If your baby's facial skin is extremely oily, a little mild soap helps dry the excess oil and pimples. Use a mild soap, preferably one like Dove or Neutrogena that contains moisturizing cream. If your baby is prone to dry skin, called eczema, use soap very sparingly and blot skin dry. Too much soap and vigorous rubbing deplete the baby's natural oils.

Q. My baby doesn't like to be held; she acts as if, when she's older, she will say to me, "Mom, as soon as I'm old enough to feed and dress myself you're fired." How can I get closer to her?

Your baby is one of the special babies whom I call noncuddly babies. The textbook baby loves to cuddle and loves to be picked up and held. However, some babies come wired with a certain temperament that makes them slow to warm up to their caregivers. This can be very frustrating to a new mother.

Above all, understand that it is not your fault. Your style of mothering does not make your baby this way; it is your baby's unique temperament. Your baby will eventually want to be held and cuddled, but perhaps not as much as other babies do. Try the following: Slow-to-warm-up babies often prefer to be carried in the forward-facing position with baby's back and head resting against your chest and your arms cradling her thighs. Your baby may arch her back and push out of your arms when being held too tightly; holding her in the facing-forward position is usually better. Around three to four months, the tonic muscle reflexes that cause the baby to hold her muscles tight and arch her back tend to relax, and she may become less stiff and easier to bend and may snuggle into the contours of your body. She may even like to be held. Try a sling-type carier that allows her to be cradled across your chest or face outward to see the world. Carriers that make her lie flat across your chest are often too confining for these babies. A gentle oil massage often helps warm up the baby so that she likes to be touched; a warm bath together often helps soothe a difficult-to-cuddle baby. Remember, go gently and gradually in loosening up this special type of baby.

Q. Is it better to put our newborn down to sleep on his stomach or his back?
Newborns usually sleep better on their stomachs than on their backs. Some mothers feel that the reason for this is that a newborn feels more helpless when awaking on his back, perhaps the way a turtle feels when turned over. When on his stomach, even a newborn has the strength to lift his head and turn himself a bit with his arms. Newborns also breathe more efficiently while lying on their stomachs. When falling asleep shortly after a feeding, your baby is best placed on her side to sleep. Roll up a towel and wedge the towel in the crevice between the baby's back and the mattress. Position your baby

on his right side; this allows his stomach to empty by gravity. After the first few weeks babies seldom remain long on their sides but roll onto their stomachs to sleep. When placing your baby down to sleep, turn her head to one side. Don't worry about her suffocating; even a newborn is able to lift her head just far enough to turn it to one side or another. Instead of placing your baby in the center of the crib, place her touching one side. Babies like the security of sleeping against some object or person; they often squirm their way into the corner of the crib as if trying to find a corner of their new womb in which to snuggle. When your baby is sleeping on his stomach, pull his legs out from under him and turn them outward. Babies tend to sleep in the fetal position with their legs tucked upward and inward under their abdomen, which tends to prolong the normal bow legged tendency in babies.

Q. Our two-week-old baby's eyes often seem to be tearing, and we have noticed yellow matter accumulating. What should we do?

Your baby probably has blocked tear ducts. Around two to three weeks of age most infants begin tearing. Normally these tears drain through a tiny canal between the nasal corner of your baby's eye and the nose. If these tear ducts are blocked, tears back up into your baby's eyes and become infected. This is not a serious problem. Try washing the yellow matter out with clear water. Gently massage with your finger tip (provided it is clean and that the fingernail has been cut very short) at the nasal corner of the eye where the lower lid meets the bridge of the nose. Massage toward the nose. Do this a half dozen times before each diaper change. If the discharge becomes thicker and yellower, consult your doctor about a prescription eye ointment to treat the infected tears. Blocked tear ducts, if properly treated, usually open up by six months. If not, an eye doctor may need to open up the tear ducts by probing into the ducts with a tiny wire. This procedure is not serious and can often be done in the doctor's office.

Q. I am afraid to cut our baby's fingernails and toenails. Help!

Sometimes babies are born with fingernails so long that they need to be cut right away to prevent the babies scratching their faces. It is easiest to trim a baby's fingernails while he is asleep. Use small, blunt-ended nail scissors especially designed for babies. A baby's toenails do not seem to grow as fast as the fingernails. You may notice that your baby's toenails seem to be ingrown at the side of his toes, but this is not a cause for concern. Because a baby's toenails are so soft and flexible, ingrown toenails are seldom a problem.

Q. Our newborn has a hard time having a bowel movement. She strains a lot, and sometimes we even notice a drop of blood on her diaper. How can we help her?

Constipation is very uncomfortable for a newborn baby, and it sounds like your baby is truly constipated. Some formula-fed babies normally have a bowel movement only once a day or once every other day but are not uncomfortable and often not constipated. Try the following: If you are formula-feeding, experiment with different formulas to see which one produces more frequent and softer stools. Formula-fed babies also need to have extra water to help the intestines form a softer stool. Watch for signs that your baby is about to have a bowel movement (drawing up of legs, facial grimaces, and signs of straining). When she begins to strain, insert a glycerine suppository (available without prescription at your drug store) into your baby's rectum and hold it there for five minutes by holding her buttocks together. This will soften the baby's stool and lubricate the rectal area to allow a smoother passage. The blood you noticed is probably due to a tiny tear, called a rectal fissure, in the lining of the rectum. These often accompany constipation. By keeping your baby's stool softer with the above dietary and stool-softening treatments, the fissure will heal within a month.

Q. Our first baby was delivered by caesarean section, and I am due soon with our next baby. It is possible to have our next baby vaginally?

Yes, a vaginal birth after caesarean is often possible. This birthing option is termed a VBAC—vaginal birth after caesarean. It used to be said that "once a caesarean, always a caesarean," but this is no longer true. Much depends on the reason for your previous section. If the reason was a problem occurring with that particular pregnancy or labor, such as breach presentation, fetal distress, or "failure to progress," then your chance of delivering your next baby vaginally is quite good. If, however, the reason for your previous section was cephalopelvic disproportion (your baby's head was too large to pass through your birth canal), then your chances of delivering your next baby vaginally may not be as good. Consult with your obstetrician concerning your chances of having a VBAC. Doctors who have had a lot of experience with VBACs have between a 60 and 80 percent success rate, but the figure varies considerably according to each mother's individual obstetrical history. Many mothers who have birthed an eight-pound baby by caesarean go on to have VBAC babies of nine pounds or more, because each pregnancy tends to widen your pelvis.

GLOSSARY

Apgar score rating system for assessing a newborn's functioning at one and five minutes after birth based on heart rate, color, muscle tone, respiration, and reflexes.

attachment parenting a parenting style that emphasizes the development of a mutually responsive and harmonious relationship between parent and child. It is characterized by feelings of rightness and completeness.

bilirubin a yellow pigment found in blood. If a newborn's liver is unable to extract the bilirubin from the extra blood cells many babies are born with, the bilirubin is deposited in the skin, leading to the condition known as normal or physiologic jaundice.

bonding process of developing a close emotional and physical attachment between parent and child that begins before birth and intensifies thereafter.

caput swelling of the scalp caused by squeezing through the birth canal.

doula helper who assists mother at home in the first few weeks of her baby's life, relieving her of all chores except mothering her baby.

fontanelle either of two soft spots on a baby's skull where bones meet. It is covered by a tough membrane.

LDR concept the use of one room for labor, birth, and recovery, with the neonate remaining with the mother unless special attention is required.

labor support person a mother with some midwifery and/or obstetrical nursing experience who assists the laboring mother.

lanugo fine hairs that may cover a newborn's back, shoulders, cheeks, and earlobes.

milia tiny, whitish bumps commonly found on the face and nose of newborns.

molding the process by which a baby's head is elongated by the movement of soft skull bones in order to fit between the mother's pelvic bones during delivery.

Mongolian spots marks resembling bruises that are frequently found on the lower backs and the buttocks of Asian, Indian, and black babies.

nevis medical term for birthmark.

newborn puberty term for slight breast enlargement in babies and, in newborn girls, the passing of a few drops of blood resembling a menstrual period, caused by excess maternal hormones that have passed through the placenta into the baby's bloodstream.

NICU neonatal intensive-care unit; a special medical unit staffed by neonatologists specially trained to care for sick newborns.

stork bites speckled reddish-pink marks often found on the upper eyelids, forehead between the eyes, and nape of the neck of newborns.

vernix white, cheesy material that covers the skin of a newborn.

INDEX

Acne, 107

ADC (Aid to Dependent Children), 139

Adopted newborn, 133–134

Age-appropriate toys, 120–121

Air travel, 143

Alcohol, 17

Allergies, formula, 63

Apgar, Virginia, 45

Apgar score, 45–46

Appearance of newborn, 38–40

Attachment parenting style, 3–7, 88–89, 139

Attachment-promoting behaviors, 35–36

Baby acne, 107

Baby Talk, 100

Bathing, 113–114

Binocular vision, 75

Birthing centers, 10

Birthmarks, 110–111

Blinking, 75

Blood tests, 46–47

Body types, 52

Bonding:
  with newborn baby, 26–32
  with preborn baby, 15–16

Bottlefeeding, 59–64

Breastfeeding, 21–22
  adopted baby, 134
  right-start techniques, 23–25

working mothers and, 145–146

Breast pump, 145

Breathing patterns, 49–50

Bumpers, crib, 96

Burping, 63–64

"Busy nest," 24–25

Caput, 39

Care of newborn:
  bathing, 113–114
  cord care, 112–113
  dressing, 116
  environmental purification, 115
  fingernails, 113
  massaging, 114
  outdoor trips, 116
  temperature regulation, 115

Carrier, 90
  selecting, 91–92

Car seats, 141–142

Car travel, 141–143

Changes in newborn:
  breathing patterns, 49–50
  excretion, 50–51
  movements, 53–55
  puberty, 51
  smiles, 52–53
  weight, 51–52

Checkups, medical, 101–103

Childbirth:
  birthing centers, 10
  home births, 10–11

LDR concept, 9
traditional methods, 8
water laboring, 11
Childbirth classes, 12–14
Circumcision, 65–69
Comforting techniques, 82–83
Contingency play, 121
Cradle cap, 107–108
Cradles, 100
Crash diets, 19
Crib safety, 95–96
Crib toys, 96
Crying:
    comfort techniques, 82–83
    response to, 4, 81–82
Cue feeding, 4, 24, 83

Demand feeding, 61
Detachment parenting style, 87–88
Dialoguing, 121–122
Diaper rash, 108–110
"Dolls' eyes," 75
Dressing, 116

Easy baby, 85–86
Ectomorphs, 52
Endomorphs, 52
Environmental purification, 115
Erythromycin, 46
Excretion, 50–51
Exercise, 19–20
Eye discharge, 104
Eye ointment, 46
Eyes, 40
Eyesight, 73–76

Face, 38
Family names, 71
Fat folds, 40

Father, postpartum period and, 57–58
Fencer's reflex, 43
Fetal alcohol syndrome, 17
Fetal awareness, 15–16
Fingernail cutting, 113
Fixating, 74–76
Fluoride supplements, 62
Fontanelle, 39
Food, nutritious, 18–19
Foreskin, 65–69
Formula-feeding, 59
    allergenicity of, 60
    amount and frequency, 60–61
    burping baby, 63–64
    choosing right formula, 62–63
    feeding schedule, 61
    vitamins and fluoride supplements, 61–62
Fussy baby, 84–85

Gag reflex, 44
Galactosemia, 47
Glossary, 164–165
Grasp reflex, 42–43
Group play, 123

Handicapped newborn, 135–137
Harmony, 15
Head of baby, 38–39
Hearing, 77–80
High need baby, 84–85
Home births, 10–11
Hormones, 149
Hospitalized newborn, 124–126
Hospital nursery, 36–37
Humidity, 115
Hypothyroidism, 46–47

Infant Massage (Schneider), 114

Iron-fortified formulas, 62

Jaundice, newborn, 47–48
Junk food, 19

Kangaroo care, 125–126
Kelly, John, 16

Labor support person, 13
Lactation consultant, 24
La Leche League International,
    14, 23
Lanugo, 39
Layette, 98–100
LDR (labor, deliver, recover)
    concept, 8
Lewis, Michael, 123
Ludington, Susan, 120

Marriage adjustments, 148–150
Massage, 114
Mattress safety, 97
Medical checkups, 101–103
Medical problems:
    eye discharge, 104
    sniffles, 105–106
    thrush, 105
Medications, pregnancy and, 17–18
Mesomorphs, 52
Milia, 107
Mobiles, 121
Mongolian spots, 111
Moro reflex, 42
Motion, 83
Movements, 53–55
Music, 16, 77

Naming baby, 70–72
Need level concept, 84, 85, 135
Neonatal intensive care unit, 9

Nesting period, 56–58
Nevi, 110–111
Newborn jaundice, 47–48
Nicotine, 17
Nursery:
    cradles, 100
    decorating, 100
    list of basics, 98–100
Nutrition, 18–19

Oil massage, 114
Outdoor trips, 116
Oxytocin, 31

Parent Infant Bonding (Klaus &
    Kennell), 26–27
Parenting style, 3–7
Periodic breathing, 49
Phenylketonuria (PKU), 46
Phimosis, 67
Postpartum depression, 130–132
Preborn baby:
    bonding with, 15–16
    mothering, 17–20
Pregnancy support groups, 14
Prickly heat, 107
Prolactin, 6, 31
Puberty, 51

Rectal fissure, 50–51
Reflexes:
    fencer's reflex (tonic neck
        reflex), 43
    gag reflex, 44
    grasp reflex, 42–43
    Moro reflex (startle response),
        42
    righting reflexes, 43
    rooting/search reflex, 41–42
    smothering avoidance reflex, 44

stepping reflex, 43–44
sucking and swallowing, 41
withdrawal reflex, 43
Righting reflexes, 43
Rooming-in, 24, 82
advantages of, 33
attachment-promoting behaviors, 35–36
compared with hospital nursery, 36–37
full, 34
modified, 34
Rooting/search reflex, 41–42

Scalp, 39
Schedule feeding, 4, 61
Schneider, Vimala, 114
Secret Life of the Unborn Child, The (Verny & Kelly), 16
Sensitivity, 6
Sharing sleep, 5
Siblings, 117–119
Sick newborn, 127–129
Singing, 122
Single mothers, 138–140
Skin, 39–40
problems of, 107–111
Skin-to-skin contact, 31, 60
Sleep/wake cycles, 7
Sling type carrier, 90–92, 143
Smegma, 66
Smiling, 52–53
Smoking, 17
Smothering avoidance reflex, 44
Sniffles, 105–106
Soft spot, 39
Speech, 78–80
Spoiling theory, 7, 87–89
Stage appropriate toys, 120–121
Startle response, 42

Stepping reflex, 43–44
Stimulation:
age and stage appropriate toys, 120–121
dialogue with baby, 121–122
group therapy, 123
individualization and, 122–123
Stimulus barrier, 77–78
Stools, 50
Stork bites, 110
Strawberry nevis, 111
Stress hormones, 15
Substitute caregiver, 147
Sucking and swallowing reflex, 41
Supplemental nursing system, 134
Support groups, 138

Talking, 78–80
Tear ducts, blocked, 104
Temperament, 84–86
Temperature, taking, 128–129
Temperature regulation, 115
Thriving, 7
Thrush, 105
Tonic neck reflex, 43
Touch, 31
Toys, appropriate, 120–121
Traditional delivery, 8
Travel:
by air, 143
by car, 141–143
travel kit, 143–144

Umbilical cord care, 112–113
Urine, 51

Vernix, 39
Verny, Thomas, 16
Vision, 73–76

Vitamin K, 47
Vitamins, 61–62

Water laboring, 11
Wearing your baby, 4–5, 82, 90
   safety tips for, 92–94
   selecting baby carrier, 91–92
Weight changes, 51–52
Weight gain, 18

Weight reduction program, 19–20
Welfare, 139
Well-baby care, 101–103
WIC (Women, Infants, and Children) program, 139
Withdrawal reflex, 43
Womanly Art of Breastfeeding, The (La Leche League), 23

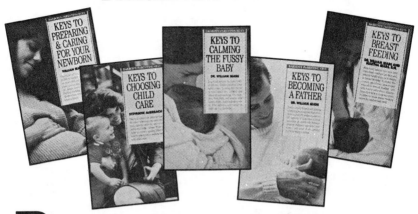

PARENTING KEYS
JUST FOR PARENTS AND
PARENTS-TO-BE!

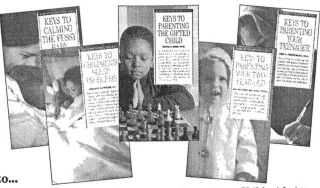

Keys to...

Adopting a Child (1925-3)

Becoming a Father (4541-6)

Breast Feeding (4540-8)

Calming the Fussy Baby (4538-6)

Child Safety and Care of
Minor Injuries (4825-3)

Childhood Illnesses (4852-0)

Children's Nutrition (4675-7)

Children's Sleep Problems (4940-3)

Choosing Childcare (4527-0)

Dealing with Childhood
Allergies (4836-9)

Dealing with Stuttering (4666-8)

Disciplining Your Young
Child (4938-1)

Investing in Your Child's
Future (4961-6)

Parenting a Child with Attention
Deficit Disorder (1459-6)

Parenting a Child with
Down Syndrome (1458-8)

Parenting the Asthmatic
Child (1677-7)

Parenting the Child with
Autism (1679-3)

Parenting the Gifted Child (1820-6)

Parenting Twins (4851-2)

Parenting Your
One-Year-Old (4772-9)

Parenting Your Teenager (4876-8)

Parenting Your
Two-Year-Old (1416-2)

Preparing and Caring for Your
Newborn (4539-4)

Preparing and Caring for
Your Second Child (4698-6)

Each Key: Paperback, $5.95 (Canada $7.95)

Books may be purchased at your bookstore, or by mail from Barron's. Enclose check or money order for total amount plus sales tax where applicable and 10% for postage and handling (minimum charge $3.75, Canada $4.00). Prices are subject to change without notice.

Barron's Educational Series, Inc.
250 Wireless Boulevard
Hauppauge, NY 11788
Call toll free: 1-800-645-3476

IN CANADA:
Georgetown Book Warehouse
34 Armstrong Avenue
Georgetown, Ontario L7G 4R9
Call toll free: 1-800-247-7160

ISBN PREFIX: 0-8120

R 4/95